P. E. COUNCIL

The Illusion
of Equality

*The Effect of Education on
Opportunity, Inequality, and Social Conflict*

Murray Milner, Jr.

The
Illusion
of
Equality

Jossey-Bass Inc., Publishers
San Francisco • Washington • London • 1972

THE ILLUSION OF EQUALITY
The Effect of Education on Opportunity,
Inequality, and Social Conflict
by Murray Milner, Jr.

Published in Great Britain by
Jossey-Bass, Inc., Publishers
St. George's House
44 Hatton Garden, London E.C.1

Library of Congress Catalogue Card Number LC 77-186584

International Standard Book Number ISBN 0-87589-129-2

Manufactured in the United States of America

JACKET DESIGN BY WILLI BAUM

FIRST EDITION

Code 7213

The Jossey-Bass
Behavioral Science Series

General Editors

WILLIAM E. HENRY
University of Chicago

NEVITT SANFORD
Wright Institute, Berkeley

Preface

The thesis of *The Illusion of Equality* is threefold. First, the expansion of education has not increased equality of opportunity in American society and will not do so in the future. Second, preoccupation with equality of opportunity is the source of many current social problems and conflicts. Third, to solve these problems we must explicitly work toward reducing economic inequality, a process which will require lowering the top as well as raising the bottom.

The initial purpose of the study that led to *The Illusion of Equality* was to estimate which forms of federal aid to higher education—student aid, grants to institutions, or tax relief to parents—contribute most to equality of opportunity. As the research progressed, I began to doubt the value of such a research focus. Gradually, I began to devote attention to basic assumptions about the relationship between student aid, educational attainment, and equality of opportunity. My new, altered focus led me to consider the role of equality of opportunity in our value system. Specifically, it led to a consideration of the significance of our commitment to equality and achievement. Only in later stages did I see how these issues might be related to basic current social problems.

The result is a picture of the role of education and equal-

ix

ity of opportunity in our society that varies from the usual assumptions. The image is a rough sketch. In some places, it is deliberately a caricature designed to emphasize qualities that have tended to be overlooked in the past. Possibly the picture is wrong, for like most broad social issues, the data relevant to the questions raised are complex and ambiguous. Nonetheless, I believe the data available support my sketch at least as well as they support traditional views. Although the picture as a whole varies from traditional views, many parts of the picture itself have been sketched before.

Part I focuses on some of the broad societal issues connected with higher education. The discussion begins with a characterization of American society as weary and frustrated and relates the social problems suggested in that characterization to the issue of equality of opportunity in higher education.

Part II is a detailed exposition of the probable effects of expanding student financial aid. Does it (as it purports to) equalize opportunities for higher education? Do the effects differ depending on whether we focus on racial inequality or social class inequality?

Part III is an analysis of the history of social conflict in twentieth-century America. It attempts to explain both the relatively low levels of conflict characteristic of the first half of the century and the conflicts of recent years in relation to the expansion of educational opportunities.

Finally, I (1) suggest that the issue of economic inequality must be faced directly and explicitly; (2) indicate how this issue will be related to educational opportunity; (3) place the suggested shift from educational opportunity to economic equality in the context of long-term historical changes; and (4) relate this analysis to traditional Marxian perspectives.

Acknowledgments

The work on *The Illusion of Equality* began in the fall of 1968 at the Bureau of Social Science Research in Washington, D.C. There I participated in a research project studying the effects of federal aid to higher education directed by Amitai Etzioni and funded by a grant from the Office of Education.

Later, the work was continued at the Center for Policy Research, New York City. Throughout this process, Dr. Etzioni has generously given his time, insights, and moral support. All three were essential and are deeply appreciated.

Part II is in large measure a summary of my doctoral dissertation for Columbia University, and I am grateful for the comments and suggestions of my dissertation defense committee, which, besides Dr. Etzioni, consisted of Sidney Aronson, Paul Ritterband, John Snook, and Sloan Wayland. During this and later stages of the work, I was also aided greatly by the comments and suggestions of my next-door neighbor, Walter Metzger.

Others who have read all or parts of the manuscript and whose helpful suggestions I have incorporated include: Arthur Kimmel, Naomi Gerstel, Robert Lindsay, Susan Riddel, Julie Millstein, Edward Lehman, Robert Bierstedt, S. M. Miller, Pamela Roby, Charles Longino, William E. Henry, and Anthony Knight. I am especially indebted to Jill Seligson, who served as my research assistant during the later stages of the work.

Most of all, the completion of this book is due to the continuing understanding, support, and assistance of my wife, Sylvia. She has devoted untold hours to typing and editing various versions of the manuscript and many more hours bolstering the often reluctant and tardy author. My daughters, Helene and Catherine, have also made the completion possible by foregoing or postponing—usually with good humor—an innumerable number of activities and projects which in their eyes needed my participation.

Despite all this assistance, a plenitude of faults undoubtedly remain, and for these I am solely responsible.

New York City   Murray Milner, Jr.
February 1972

Contents

xiii

THREE: EDUCATION, SOCIAL CONFLICT,
AND SOCIAL CHANGE

The Illusion
of Equality

*The Effect of Education on
Opportunity, Inequality, and Social Conflict*

Status Inflation

One

Americans are tired. A general weariness pervades our individual and collective lives. But the malaise which characterizes our society is not, however, simply the debility of overexertion. Intertwined with the enervation is a strong sense of frustration, a feeling that despite strong commitments and great efforts our purposes remain unfulfilled, that the payoff we expected has not materialized.

We are frustrated by the interminable war in Indochina, by air which hurts our eyes, by spending hours each week creeping along overcrowded "expressways" or being mashed into buses and subway cars, by the paradox of higher prices and greater unemployment. We are bored with voting for politicians who promise one thing and do another. We are sick of white racism and black power, of innumerable campus protests, and blatant government harassment of dissent. We are wearied by our loss of community and the resulting loneliness. Yet at

1

the same time we are tired of being too close to one another—
whether through our paper-thin apartment walls or in the con-
gestion of our national parks. We are scared by increasing levels
of crime and violence and perturbed at the erosion of civil
liberties.

Weariness and Frustration

Most of the factors mentioned above wear on all Americans. No one enjoys polluted air or bumper to bumper traffic.
But in addition to common problems, special kinds of weariness
and frustration are concentrated in only certain sectors of our
society.

There is the weariness and frustration of *the excluded:*
blacks, Appalachian miners, Chicano migrants, American Indians, and women. Such frustration comes from knowing that
the dice are loaded against you and that there is no other game
in town. For the excluded, frustration runs high because the injustices are clearest and greatest.

There is the weariness and frustration of *the vulnerable,*
the majority of Americans who believe they have a meaningful
stake in the system: the upper class, the middle class, and the
"respectable" working class. These people are vulnerable not
because they have been excluded, but because of the nature of
their inclusion. They have been immersed in America. They
have worked, sacrificed, fought, and died for it. They feel
frustrated and used up not because their unending effort has
tired them, but because their successes are less satisfying than
they had anticipated. But they are reluctant to admit this, even
to themselves. This frustration is exacerbated because others—
especially their children—increasingly reject the product of their
life's labor. Although the vulnerable know that the society they
have wrought is far from perfect, they cannot believe that it
can fail to be something of value. They are tired of being told
about the exploitative effects of what they know to be altruistic
efforts. They are both wearied and frustrated by arguing and
bickering with their children about values which seem self-
evident. They are heartsick over increasing profanity, desecrated
flags, vulgar dress, unkempt hair, and arrogant youth. Their

debilitating fatigue is the result of fear and anxiety; and their fear comes from the knowledge that despite their best efforts, what they most believe in is increasingly insecure and vulnerable.

There is the weariness and frustration of *the chosen*. This weariness is not limited to but is concentrated in the children of the affluent. They have been chosen for privilege, the privilege of having fathers with stature and responsibility— fathers who know everything about their job except its importance, who give the chosen everything they need but companionship. But the chosen neither chose their privilege nor worked for it. They take it for granted and increasingly they seem to tire of it. They are disgusted by the products and advertising of the consumer society. They are sick of being drafted to fight a war that they are convinced is unjust and immoral. They are weary of adult hypocrisy about race, sex, and drugs. They are increasingly frustrated by their seeming inability to do anything about these issues.

They are especially exhausted from and dismayed by simply watching the endless striving—the fixation to move ever onward and upward. The chosen are bored with their affluence and profoundly puzzled by their parents' seeking after greater riches, which have so obviously failed to satisfy them in the past.

But maybe most of all the chosen are wearied and frustrated by the environment in which they spend most of their daytime hours: the school, our nursery for endless striving. They are tired of the nursery's tedium and conformity. They do, of course, experience moments of light and even joy, but such moments are infrequent. If nothing else, the length of time they must spend in school is enough to wear out all but the most hearty. They are subjected to a minimum of sixteen years of continual processing by the educational bureaucracies. The average time for the chosen is probably several years longer. During this time, they are repeatedly instructed, tested, counseled, graded, sorted. However, social pressures force them to more than passively submitting to this process. They must also become committed to endless striving. They must learn to believe in study, work, grading, effort, sorting, and promotion. Otherwise they will not be allowed to continue their education.

Neither will they be prepared for the competition and struggle of the adult world. Only if we perceive the extent to which our society is impregnated with endless striving—both at home and in the schools—can we adequately comprehend the weariness and frustration of the chosen.

What are the sources of our weariness and frustration? My first premise is that an understanding of our problems can be derived from considering the consequences of endless striving—especially its effects on the relationship between the excluded, the vulnerable, and the chosen.

The vulnerable are wearied both because they have put forth a great deal of real effort and work and because the payoff has not been as satisfying as they expected. They are frustrated because their endless striving, their accomplishments, and the legitimacy of both, have at best been unappreciated and they are being increasingly rejected with open derision.

The excluded reject the efforts of the vulnerable because they know what the vulnerable sense, but cannot admit: that the game was rigged. The winnings of the vulnerable are due at least as much to the dice being loaded in their favor as to their very real endless striving. The excluded see that for them endless striving is pointless striving and that for the vulnerable, it is something less than a pure commitment to moral virtue. Consequently, the excluded are weary because of the energy required to keep from falling further behind. They are frustrated because they know that through no fault of their own they cannot win.

The chosen reject endless striving for three reasons. First, they are disgusted by the hypocrisy of the vulnerable in their dealings with the excluded. Second, they see that even when you play with the game rigged in your favor, the cost of endless striving is greater than any conceivable prize. But most of all, they reject it because they have seen the actual prizes and they know that winning is losing. The chosen are fatigued by the process of watching the game and preparing for it in the nursery. They are frustrated at the thought of having to devote their lives to what appears to them a meaningless game.

If my first premise is that a clearer understanding of our

weariness and frustration can be obtained by focusing on the consequences of endless striving, my second premise is that the nature, sources, and consequences of endless striving can be more clearly seen if we focus on the role of the nursery. Our schools are not the primary cause of our problems although they are an important contributing factor. However, an analysis of the role of education helps to clarify the sources of our endless striving and the nature of our current malady.

In the following discussion the reader should keep in mind that my image of weariness and frustration should not be taken too literally; it is not intended as a detailed and precise sociological description. Rather, this image is a simplified characterization of the complex social problems which plague our society and the ethos or spirit which seems to have resulted from our inability to arrive at meaningful solutions. Weariness and frustration are intended to remind the reader of the existential realities which confront us daily and to set the stage for the analysis which follows.

Endless Striving

Before turning to an analysis of the nursery, we need to look more closely at the nature of our endless striving; it can be better understood in relation to the process of status inflation. Economic inflation is the increase in the supply of symbols (money) without a parallel real increase in what the symbols stand for (goods and services). Consequently the value of the symbols decreases. Consider a thousand loaves of bread and a total money supply of one hundred dollars. If men buy and sell nothing but bread, the price of each loaf is ten cents. But if the money supply is suddenly increased to two hundred dollars with no change in the quantity of bread available, the bread costs twenty cents a loaf. The price of bread has become inflated, or to turn it around, the real exchange value of each unit of money has decreased.

Inflation can occur, however, on another level. This second level is not economic inflation but social inflation or, more accurately, status inflation. Status inflation occurs when there is a decrease in the social value attributed to a given objective

amount of resources. The most obvious example is a decrease
in the amount of social status attributed to any given level of
absolute income. For example, in 1900 a man who made six
thousand dollars was perceived as being much richer (nearer
the top of the income distribution) than the man who makes
six thousand dollars today—even when the value of the dollar
is held constant.

The same phenomenon obviously occurs with respect to
other resources—for instance, type of occupation. In 1950, professional and technical workers made up 7 or 8 per cent of the
labor force. But this figure had doubled to 15 per cent by 1970.
In the same period, the percentage of white-collar workers
shifted from 37 per cent to 50 per cent. In all probability, this
inflation will eventually decrease the social status traditionally
accorded these groups. However, the available data are not without ambiguities. On the one hand, studies of the ranking of
various occupations show a high degree of stability over time
and between cultures. However, such rankings indicate only
that occupation A has a higher status than B, B higher than C,
and so on. They do not indicate whether the distance between
A and B or even the value of both have decreased. On the other
hand, a professional occupation must upgrade its level of expertise to maintain its prestige, and the inflationary process may
possibly be offset or obscured by the tendency toward greater
professionalization. There seems to be a necessity for professional occupations to either upgrade the level of their expertise
or to be replaced by similar but higher status occupations. For
example, most physicians were general practitioners before
World War II, although most recent graduates of medical
school now have a specialty. Apparently the general practitioners have suffered a reduction in status as a result of this trend.
A similar "replacement process" seems to have occurred for
numerous occupations: bookkeepers have been replaced by ac-
countants, salesmen have become sales representatives, anesthe-
tists have been replaced by anesthesiologists, maintenance men
have become engineers. The relative slowness of change in
occupational status and the countervailing tendency in most
occupations toward greater professionalization may explain why

the effect of the inflationary process is less evident in this sector than elsewhere.

The inflationary process is particularly apparent in the relationship between consumer commodities and status symbols. As new kinds of consumer goods—especially durable goods—come onto the market, they frequently become the symbol of middle-class affluence. However, when the item becomes widely distributed it loses its symbolic significance and is replaced by another product, usually a more expensive one. The most obvious examples of this process were the television set and hi-fi in the 1950s rapidly replaced by the color set and stereo in the 1960s, only to be outmoded by the quadrasonic sound system and video tape recorder in the 1970s.

A similar process occurs in the realm of education. In 1950, one third of the population over twenty-five had a high school diploma. By 1970, three quarters of the population were high school graduates.[1] Obviously, the relative social (and economic value) of a high school diploma has decreased. Jobs which at one time required a high school education now require a college education.

The fact that status inflation occurs is fairly obvious. But what of its consequences? One consequence is its stimulation of endless striving. In American society, social status is closely linked with income, occupation, education, and consumption. If some steadily increase their absolute level of income, education, and consumption and shift into more prestigious jobs, others have the alternative of following suit or accepting a reduction in social status. One of the most widely accepted propositions in sociology is that people try to avoid reductions in their status. As a result, most people are motivated to further striving in order to maintain their social position.

At this point, let us note the difference between endless striving and status inflation. Endless striving is an attitudinal and behavioral characteristic of individuals. The number of individuals who engage in striving may vary from none to all,

[1] US Bureau of the Census, *Statistical Abstract of the United States: 1970*, p. 110.

depending on the particular society. Status inflation is a social
process and is an attribute of a society, not of individuals by
themselves. Status inflation cannot occur unless a large percentage of the population is involved in the process. Status inflation
transforms initial individual impulses for achievement into endless striving. That is, status inflation continually erodes away
the status quo and the psychological satisfactions acquired by
improving resources. This erosion leads to more striving by the
individual. When a large percentage of the population so strive,
the result is additional status inflation and the cycle begins again.
Because of this seesaw relationship, an attempt to assign causal
priority to one of these factors is meaningless. Rather, the important thing to see is how their interaction produces a spiral
of status inflation.

Status Seeking and Equality of Opportunity

From Alexis de Tocqueville and Thorstein Veblen to
David Riesman, Vance Packard, or Charles Reich, commentators
on our society have always observed that Americans are unusually preoccupied with raising the level of their social status.
In his classic *Democracy in America*, Tocqueville noted: "The
first thing that strikes one in the United States is the innumerable crowd of those striving to escape from their original social
condition. . . . Every American is eaten up with longing to
rise. . . . All are constantly bent on gaining property, reputa-
tion, and power." [2]

At the same time, America has been noted for being an
unusually egalitarian society in the sense that we are relatively
unconcerned about the status of others in our day-to-day interactions. It is not accepted behavior to be haughty toward those
with low social status or to give special deference to those with
high social status. Americans are not overly threatened by in-
teracting with those of lower status nor overly awed by inter-
acting with those of higher status. In this sense, we treat one
another in a more or less equal fashion. Tocqueville observed:
"In America . . . privileges of birth never existed and . . .
wealth brings its possessors no peculiar right. . . . Their man-

[2] A. de Tocqueville, *Democracy in America*, p. 627.

ner therefore is natural, frank, and open. One sees that there
is practically nothing they either hope or fear from each other
and that they are not concerned to show or hide their social
position." [3]

American attitudes toward social status are, of course,
relative. We have traditionally been more concerned with raising our own status and less status conscious in our interactions
with others than have those in most other societies. Americans
are not the only ones who try to raise their social status, nor
are we wholly oblivious to status differences in our treatment
of others.

How does this peculiar combination of relatively high
concern about our own social status and relatively low concern
about the social status of others come about? [4] One of the primary factors is our strong emphasis on equality of opportunity.
Probably more than any other society—certainly more than
any other capitalist society—we stress equality of opportunity
as an ideal. Moreover, we are constantly instituting new programs which purport to bring the reality closer to this ideal.

In order to understand how emphasis on equality of
opportunity leads to status seeking, it is necessary to make
explicit one of the structural characteristics which is a prerequisite to such an emphasis. Ironically enough, for equality of
opportunity to be emphasized, there must be a significant degree
of inequality. If everyone were equal (had virtually the same
income, political influence, and prestige), equality of opportunity would occur automatically, and this issue would receive
scant attention. Only when the rewards of a society are dis-

[3] Tocqueville, p. 567. Foreign observers like Tocqueville have frequently noted this characteristic. For an overview of such observations
see S. M. Lipset, *The First New Nation*, pp. 125f.

[4] See Lipset and H. Zetterberg for an exegesis and elaboration of
Thorstein Veblen's analysis of the sources of status seeking. (S. M. Lipset and R. Bendix, *Social Mobility in the Industrial Society*, pp. 60–63.)
Their discussion emphasizes the universality of status seeking while this
discussion—and Veblen's own discussion—focus on the characteristics of
America which accentuate an admittedly universal phenomenon. Lipset
has also focused on the more uniquely American sources of this phenomenon in a line of argument very similar to the one to be presented
here. See *The First New Nation*. Lipset notes similar analyses have been
offered by Tocqueville and other European observers.

tributed in an unequal fashion does it make any sense for people
to be concerned about having a fair chance to compete for the
prizes.

In a society with a significant amount of inequality,
placing stress on equality of opportunity is intended to give
everyone a chance to win the highest rewards. What a person
receives is not supposed to be affected by factors over which
he has no control—for instance, the social status of his parents.
The highest rewards are supposed to go to those who achieve
the most, irrespective of who their parents were. Everybody
is given a chance to get ahead, to raise his social status. But
such a stratification system is a two sided coin with an unintended but an inevitable corollary: everyone can also lose social status. Status insecurity is a necessary part of a society
which has both significant inequality and equality of opportunity. Such insecurity usually produces anxiety. Hence we see
how equality of opportunity produces the combination of anxiety about one's own status but a deemphasis on the status
consciousness toward others. Stressing equality of opportunity
necessarily makes the status structure fluid and the position of
individual within it ambiguous and insecure.

In such a situation, the only defense is a good offense.
Trying to keep those below you from improving their position
is not legitimate (and frequently impractical). Consequently,
the most obvious strategy is to try to stay ahead. If others raise
their income or education level, you must raise yours. If they
get a new car, you must get a bigger one. The result is status
inflation.

Briefly, I am arguing that equality of opportunity necessarily produces status insecurity; status insecurity encourages
status seeking; and the three of them combine to produce status
inflation. This idea is certainly not new, and several social commentators have presented similar analyses. A number of years
ago, Werner Sombart, the famous German economic historian,
made the following observation: "Since all are seeking success,
. . . everyone is forced into a struggle to beat every other
individual; and a steeplechase begins . . . that differs from all
other races in that the goal is not fixed but constantly moves

even further away from the runners." [5] Such a race is necessarily tiring. Extended indefinitely, it could lead to exhaustion and collapse.

Our next task is to try to elucidate how such a race got under way, or more specifically, how we have come to place such an emphasis on equality of opportunity.

Achievement and Equality

In his famous study of the race problem in the U.S., Gunnar Myrdal observed that Americans are caught in a dilemma. The dilemma is the result of a basic contradiction in American society, a contradiction between what he called the American creed, which emphasizes equality for all, and the well established caste system, in which Negroes are treated as second-class citizens and inferior human beings. Americans had to choose between these contradictory elements because the ideology of racial inferiority and the passivity of the Negroes—the two things which made possible maintenance of the contradiction—were fast eroding. The contradiction to which Myrdal pointed was between ideas and behavior, and the dilemma was whether we would choose to be true to our ideals, or would forsake them for antithetical patterns of behavior.

But America has been confronted with a basic dilemma on another level, one based not so much on a contradiction between ideals and actions as on the tension between two sets of partially contradictory basic ideals. This contradiction is not primarily between the American creed and American behavior, but between elements of the creed itself.

Seymour Martin Lipset describes this contradiction in terms of a tension between the value of equality and the value of achievement.[6] By equality Lipset means "that we believe all

---

[5] Quoted by Lipset in *The First New Nation*, p. 129. See also Tocqueville, especially pp. 531, 536–537.

[6] I do not argue that the two values are totally contradictory. Lipset would probably put more stress on their congruence and less on their incompatability than I do, but this is a difference in emphasis, for he comments, "These values, though related, are not entirely compatible; each has given rise to reactions which threaten the other" (*The First New Nation*, pp. 1–2).

persons must be given respect simply because they are human
beings; we believe that the differences between high- and low-
status people reflect accidental, and perhaps temporary, variations
in social relationships. . . . Achievement is a corollary to our
belief in equality. For people to be equal, they need to have a
chance to become equal. . . . Achievement is a function of
equality of opportunity." [7]

Lipset is correct in identifying equality and achievement
as central to our value system. However, I would prefer to
state the relationship between the two in a slightly different
manner. If anything, equality is a derivative of achievement
rather than vice versa. Our commitment to achievement is primary, and our commitment to equality is in large measure a
result of the former.[8] At the very least, achievement is on a par
with equality. Moreover—and here is the important point—
equality of opportunity is probably best understood as a mechanism for compromising and reconciling the contradictory aspects
of equality and achievement. Although the historical origins of
our emphasis on equality of opportunity are complex, I believe
that considering it as the product of such a compromise is a
useful and not inaccurate analytical simplification. (For formal
definitions of the concepts of achievement and equality see the
appendix at the end of this chapter.)

Americans genuinely believe in equality—at least to the
extent that most societies believe in the values they profess. At
the same time, we emphasize the right and virtue of individual
achievement; the rewards and privileges that a person receives
should be closely related to his accomplishments or at the very
least to his efforts. Obviously, the achievements of people differ.

---

[7] Lipset, *The First New Nation*, p. 2.

[8] From a historical point of view, the demands of the bourgeoisie
for equality were primarily a rejection of inherited privileges supported
by law. They rejected these features of feudalism not so much because
of an abstract commitment to equality but because of an increasingly
concrete commitment to achievement. Feudal privileges restricted the
nature and scope of their economic activities and prevented them from
translating their already considerable economic achievements into other
forms of social status. See R. H. Tawney, *Equality*, pp. 91–100.

Consequently, we cannot follow the second principle—rewards according to achievement—and maintain the first principle, equality. We have reconciled these two values by saying that, at the beginning of the race, everybody should be allowed to line up on the same starting line, but that the race is for real and those running the fastest deserve to win. This principle is what we mean by equality of opportunity and provides a way out of the dilemma of choosing between equality and achievement.

There are at least two problems, however, with the "fair race" model. First, real life is not analogous to a single running of the hundred-yard dash. It is analogous, rather, to an endless relay race. Whether you are ahead when you finish your lap is strongly influenced by how far ahead or behind your team was when you were handed the baton. Of course, we are aware of this problem, and at the beginning of each new lap we offer some extra help to those who have to start behind. But this extra help always seems to take the form of a consolation prize. (Some of the recent consolation prizes include such programs as Project Head Start, the Job Corps, and Upward Bound.) And as with most consolation prizes, they are considerably smaller than the prizes that go to those who actually come in ahead. If the men who must start the second lap from behind get some extra coaching and encouragement from the minor officials who referee the race, the men whose team is ahead have had years of attention from the best coaches that are available. Thus, the first problem with the fair race as a model for equality of opportunity is that in real life there is no clear-cut beginning or end to the competition. The handicaps or advantages existing at the start of each new lap are extremely difficult to change.

But the first deficiency is based on a second problem with this model, or rather with the way we have traditionally applied it to our collective life. In our economic and social activities, we have acted as though winning were dependent upon how hard the individual tried—assuming the race was "fair." That is, we have seen achievement primarily in terms of individual effort. If people were given an equal chance at the beginning, their final destination would be determined by how hard they chose to work. How hard one worked was seen as a thing which each individual could control. Therefore, it was perfectly fair to reward those who chose to put out the most effort. (I can remember quite clearly being told at home, and even to a greater extent at school, that "you can do anything or be anything you want bad enough.")

This image of social justice, however, assumes a person whose actions are in large measure determined by an inner will, a person who has a high degree of freedom to choose between the alternatives that confront him. But just as we have come to see that life is more like a relay race than the hundred-yard dash, we have, during the twentieth century, increasingly changed our image of man. We have not done away with his individual freedom, but we have reduced it and increasingly attribute his actions not to his unrestricted free will but to his location in the social environment. We view an individual's criminal actions in the context of a background of poverty; we see an executive's alcoholism as linked to occupational stress and a nagging wife; insanity is now an illness and is usually seen as a result of external pressure (past or present) rather than internal moral weakness. If we still believe in individual freedom and responsibility—and we do—we believe in it much less than we did in the past.

Consequently, we are less sure about how people should be rewarded and punished for their behavior. We no longer assume that old people who did not save when they were young have no right to expect an adequate standard of living in their old age. We are not quite as sanguine about taxing individuals who make millions of dollars a year at the same rate as those who have meager incomes. Nor do we feel free to be openly indifferent if large numbers of college students flunk out. I am not arguing that in practice we make adequate provision for the old, that the rich pay their fair share of the taxes, or that students who have academic difficulties receive adequate help. I am arguing, however, that generally our ideals no longer justify such patterns. In academic terms, the ethic of social Darwinism has

been significantly muted if not eradicated. This modification in
our ethic of justice is due largely to our revised image of the
individual. Formally he is still master of his ship, but we are
increasingly aware that his fate is strongly influenced by winds
and currents over which he has no control as an individual.

To summarize, our commitment to the ideal of equality
of opportunity as a means of balancing our beliefs in equality
and our beliefs in achievement was based upon a certain image
of man. This image pictured the individual as an autonomous
being who was therefore in large measure personally responsible
for how much or how little he achieved (and therefore received).
The old image of man made equality of opportunity a relatively
stable compromise between equality and achievement. But because the old image has been eroded, the old compromise is no
longer stable. Consequently, we are confronted with a dilemma:
we must choose whether we will place greater emphasis on
achievement or on equality in the future.

Those who are familiar with the way our penal system
operates or those who must attempt to convince the business
community to support reform and expansion of the welfare
system may be more than a little dubious that a new image of
man has arrived or that social Darwinism has been dethroned.
Nevertheless, such a change is on the horizon. More accurately,
it is present, but in a sense deliberately overlooked. But the trend
is like the development of corns or bunions. At first, people tend
to overlook them and walk on, or they treat them with cheap and
painless home remedies. Eventually, the problem can no longer
be ignored and the individual must choose between painful treatment or incapacitation. The dilemma we face is similar. We
cannot ignore the instability of the present compromise between
equality and achievement much longer. Meaningful treatment is
going to be painful. Procrastination may be fatal.

A postscript is required. If those of Marxist persuasion
have bothered to read this far, they are undoubtedly frustrated,
if not disgusted. My attempt to explain the American emphasis
on equality of opportunity in terms of a compromise between
the contradictory aspects of our value on equality and our value

on achievement will appear to them hopelessly idealistic—in both
the philosophical and moral sense. Such an analysis ignores what
for the Marxist is a much more important causal relationship—the
effect of economic interest on American ideology. From this
perspective, our emphasis on equality of opportunity is seen
primarily as an ideology used to support the existing structures
of inequality and to provide a rationale for the upgrading of the
occupational structure, which is essential to the continued viability of our capitalist system. But these two interpretations are not
contradictory. If economic development had not created large
numbers of white-collar and professional jobs, the rate of upward
mobility we have experienced in the last hundred years would
not have been possible. Moreover, the belief in the existence and
desirability of equality of opportunity would have undoubtedly
paled if economic development had not produced high rates of
upward mobility.

But most European countries have experienced similar
rates of economic development and upward mobility. Consequently, our strong emphasis on equality of opportunity cannot
be explained simply in terms of economic factors. Both the
tension between the value emphases on equality and achievement
and the high level of economic development seem to have been
necessary conditions for our particular preoccupation with equality of opportunity. Neither factor was a sufficient condition in
itself.

Now we are ready to consider the role that education has
played in these broad social processes.

*Appendix: A Note on the Concepts of
Equality and Achievement*

Since these concepts are a basic part of the analysis, a
more elaborate specification of their meaning and interrelation-
ship must be provided.

First, let me try to clarify what I am attempting to define.
Clyde Kluckhohn defines values as "abstract standards that tran-
scend the impulses of the moment and ephemeral situations." [9]

---

[9] C. Kluckhohn, *Culture and Behavior*, p. 289.

I am trying to specify, in a slightly more detailed way, the content of two particular sets of standards or values—those sets of standards which Lipset has summarized under the terms of equality and achievement. The problem is to specify what standards Americans have in fact held in these two areas referred to as equality and achievement.

A number of difficulties are involved in such a task. First, a great deal of variation is always present between groups and individuals. Second, the content of such standards tends to change over time. We can, however, define central tendencies, namely, the predominant view. I shall try to identify these traditional central tendencies. To carry out this task adequately would be a major piece of historical research in itself. I have not attempted this. Instead, what follows is a weak substitute. It is an impressionistic attempt to specify the traditional content of these values by one who is a participant in the social system under consideration. The justification for attempting this task is not my own competence to carry it out, but rather the need to clarify the assumptions which underlie the rest of my analysis. The purpose of this exercise is to allow the reader to judge the validity of these assumptions and consequently the adequacy of the analysis based upon them.

Probably the easiest way to begin the specification of the traditional meaning of *equality* is to indicate what it has not meant. When Americans have advocated equality, they have not meant that wealth and power were to be equally distributed. What they have meant seems to center on two issues. First they have felt that all citizens should be treated the same with regard to certain basic rights: sufferage; the right to buy, sell, or hold property; the right to participate in politics and hold public office; the right to be represented by a lawyer when accused of crime; the right to trial by jury; and so on.[10] All citizens have not in fact been equal in their abilities to actualize these basic rights. But we have traditionally considered illegitimate attempts by the

---

[10] None of this discussion applies to blacks because traditionally, we have not, as a nation, believed in equality for blacks. The discussion is limited to the standards that whites have applied to one another.

state or other citizens to curtail these basic rights, or attempts by the individual to gain special privileges in the areas of these basic rights.

A second focus is in the realm of respect and dignity. (Lipset's concern is with this dimension.) Despite differences in power, wealth, and occupational status, all individuals are to be accorded a basic respect and dignity. This principle applies particularly to our casual day-to-day interactions. Those with wealth and power cannot legitimately demand deferential treatment such as special forms of address, titles, or even a subservient manner. A more technical way of saying this is that compared to most other countries there has tended to be a low correlation between wealth and power on the one hand and respect and deference on the other hand.

While the primary task is to identify the "traditional central tendency," a word about historical trends is appropriate here. The general trend seems to be toward an erosion of equal respect and dignity. As our society has become complex and mobile, individuals find it increasingly difficult to be aware of one another's more personal characteristics that might offset respect accorded to wealth, power, and occupational status. A basic respect given to all, irrespective of other inequalities, may in large measure reflect a frontier society which no longer exists. An excerpt from an article on families that moved to Alaska in 1959 to homestead illustrates the point:

"Once you've been here you don't want to go back," said Eleanor Bubino, an energetic, sharp featured woman who manages the restaurant while her husband tends bar. "They don't change—you change. I can't explain it. Down there in the United States you have to follow a certain path. Here people don't take you for your money or your profession. They take you for your person, for yourself. You don't have to have possessions to be somebody." "People are more relaxed here," added Mrs. Sik. "I don't think anybody judges anybody else like they do outside." [11]

[11] *The New York Times*, March 24, 1971.

While there may have been a significant decrease in this aspect of equality, compared to most other societies America is relatively egalitarian in this regard.[12]

On the other hand, a trend toward expanding the concept of basic rights has apparently developed. Relatively early in our history certain basic levels of education were at least implicitly included. With the welfare state of the New Deal, old age pensions and security against unemployment came to be added. The current debate is over health care and minimum levels of income. Whether there is a causal connection between these two apparent trends is an interesting question requiring empirical research.

To summarize: By equality I mean the equal basic rights and equal respect we accord each other as human beings. In the long run, there has been a tendency toward the extension of basic rights and the erosion of equal respect.

Let us now turn our attention to achievement. A value such as achievement can be actualized in a society on at least three levels. The first is the level of motivation: do people have a strong desire to do well? The second is the level of performance: do people in fact perform well? This second level is influenced by factors other than motivation such as tools and available resources. The third level is the social reward system: are people differentially rewarded for differential performance? [13] We are concerned primarily with this third level. To what extent and in what ways have Americans traditionally subscribed to the idea that those who perform best should be rewarded most? Clearly, reward for performance has been a very

---

[12] John Kenneth Galbraith suggests that the obedience and servility of the lower classes has decreased as a result of the general increase in the level of living. However, his discussion seems to focus on a type of deferential behavior which has probably been comparatively rare in our society, except possibly among minority groups. *The Affluent Society*, p. 77.

[13] The effects of various degrees and types of articulation between these three levels involve a major empirical and theoretical question, and much of the debate over the sources of modernization revolves around this issue.

strong tradition within our society; it is integrally tied to the widespread emphasis on competition. There have, of course, been minority reports which called for a radical form of equality: religious communities such as Oneida, populist movements such as Huey Long's "every man a king" program, and Marxist groups like the Communists and the Progressive Labor Party. But these have been relatively rare and have seldom had any extended impact upon the society as a whole.

Now that an attempt has been made to specify the traditional normative meaning of equality and achievement, we must clarify how these values conflict with one another. First, there is admittedly relatively little conflict on a logical level. Equality and achievement, as we have specified them, are not mutually exclusive possibilities. For example, unequal monetary rewards coupled with equal respect and dignity is a logical possibility. The conflict is primarily on the empirical level. In the real world, it is difficult to break the link between such things as an individual's wealth, power, and occupational status on the one hand and the respect that an individual is accorded on the other hand. The legitimate inequalities of the first realm seem to lead almost inevitably to illegitimate inequalities in the second realm. Moreover, the combination of these legitimate inequalities (wealth, power, and so on) and illegitimate inequalities (respect and dignity) affects the extent to which individuals are able to actualize their basic rights, for example, participation in politics and meaningful legal defense when accused of crime.

In many ways, I believe we are aware of this contradiction. The response to this realization has been twofold. First, the contradiction is denied. This response is probably most typical of those who benefit from the contradiction. The second response has been to stress the impermanence of the inequalities—both the legitimate and the illegitimate ones—by placing an emphasis on equality of opportunity. This response is common to both the privileged and the underprivileged.

God, Mother, Country, and Schools

Two

Supposedly, every boy scout and most Americans in general honor "God, mother, and country." Those of cynical disposition might contend that these have traditionally been revered primarily because of the self-serving but energetic efforts of ministers, mothers, and politicians. But whatever the source of their importance as patriotic liturgy, religion, the family, and the political system have historically played a central role in American society. But there is nothing unusual in this; these social patterns are central to nearly all societies. If we have been creative or ingenious, it is in ceremoniously praising the virtues of these institutions, not in giving them a more central role than they are given in most societies.

There is, however, a social institution not included in the above formulation of the boy scout trinity: an institution to which we have given almost as much praise and certainly an importance unique to America—formal education. If most societies have traditionally held God, mother, and country in esteem, only Americans have held such a high faith in the power and virtue of education in general and the school in particular. At least since the Jacksonian period, and some would argue earlier, we have emphasized the importance of popular education for democracy. It has been, and still is, argued that democracy can only work if the masses have a high level of education which enables them to inform themselves on political and social issues. Moreover, in the main we have relied on the school to provide this educational base.

But in addition to the general task of citizenship education, we have relied on our schools to help solve innumerable special problems. The schools were, for instance, a primary means of acculturating the waves of immigrants that arrived in the nineteenth and early twentieth centuries. We have used our formal school system not only to teach the three Rs, the humanities, and the sciences, but also to train homemakers, farmers, auto mechanics, cabinet makers, and professional athletes. In the late 1950s, when Russia startled the world with Sputnik, one of our first reactions was to call for school reform and increase government expenditures on education. In the middle of the 1960s, driver education was the most rapidly growing area of secondary schools, and according to Lawrence Cremin educators argued that: "Fifty thousand people a year are being killed on the highways; obviously, traditional forms of driving instruction are not working; some new institution must assume the responsibility; the school must do it." Cremin notes, "it is a curious solution, requiring courses instead of seat belts, but typically American." [1] More recently, the education system has been called upon to provide sex education and even birth control information. Currently, our schools are being assigned a major role in dealing with the epidemic of drug abuse among high school, college, and even

[1] L. Cremin, *The Genius of American Education*, p. 10.

elementary school students. In short, we seem to have faith that education will solve almost any social problem. Cremin quotes one of his friends as saying that when other countries have critical social problems, the result is a revolution; in America, we organize a new course.[2]

America is unique in the extent to which it has relied on formal education to inculcate values and actualize goals. Moreover, this reliance seems especially strong with respect to our emphasis on achievement and equality.

Whether the American educational system emphasizes individual achievement more than the elitist systems of Europe is debatable. It seems definite, however, that American schools place a strong emphasis on achievement and competition, and that they have been a major social mechanism in the maintenance of this value emphasis. Moreover, they have had extended access to a much higher percentage of the population than have the educational systems of other countries. Therefore schools have an opportunity to instill the achievement ethic into a high percentage of our population.

If some of the elite school systems of other nations may have emphasized achievement more than the U.S. system, there is no doubt that America has over the past hundred and fifty years had the world's most egalitarian school system.[3] It has been egalitarian both in its curriculum and educational philosophy, and in its accessability to the great majority of our population. As a result of this joint emphasis on achievement and equality, our schools have faced the same dilemma as our society as a whole: how to maximize and reconcile two values which are in large measure contradictory. There have been at least two related consequences of this tension. With respect to educational philosophy and curriculum, schools have shifted their emphasis from achievement and content to egalitarianism and human relations, and then back to achievement. The most recent phases of this cycle

2 Cremin, p. 10.
3 Some of the socialist countries such as Cuba and China may currently have more egalitarian systems than the U.S. However, we certainly have the longest tradition of emphasizing equality in the educational system.

were illustrated by the emphasis on academic rigor immediately following Sputnik contrasted with the current trend toward heterogeneous groupings and community control.[4] Put in a slightly different way, the first consequence of the achievement-equality tension has had to do with how students were treated when they were participants in the educational system—an internal struggle.

The second consequence of the tension between equality and achievement has been related to the scope of the educational system and who gets to participate in the system—an external struggle. As our knowledge becomes more extensive and our economy more complex, those inclined toward high achievement have sought and obtained higher and higher levels of formal education. But before long, social pressure developed to expand the higher levels of education in order to make access to this level of training available to a larger and larger portion of the population. We have repeatedly expanded our educational facilities to meet the demands for greater equality of opportunity. Just as in the society as a whole, the educational system has tried to reconcile the tension between achievement and equality by providing equality of opportunity.

But the stress on equality of opportunity within the educational system has greater significance than simply being an illustration of a process which occurs within many sectors of our society. We have relied primarily on the educational sector to bring about the actualization of equality of opportunity in all sectors of our society. We have in large measure assumed that if individuals had a chance to increase their level of education, they would necessarily improve their opportunities with respect to occupational status and income. Consequently, most of our efforts toward improving equality of opportunity have focused

---

[4] I do not mean to imply that the history of educational curriculum in the United States can be interpreted simply as a shifting, cyclical emphasis on achievement versus equality. This cycle has, however, been an important theme, though the long-term trend has probably been toward greater equality. Nor do I mean to imply that the advocates of community control are unconcerned about achievement or academic standards. They are concerned, however, with raising the performance of those who in the past have been "low-achievers," and much less with developing "top performance" for an academic elite.

on educational opportunity and have involved expansion of the school system.

Let us here mention briefly the historical relationship between education and the demand for greater equality. The most diverse subcultures in America have all supported education as the means to their own particular visions of society. By 1650, both Massachusetts and Connecticut required that all towns with a hundred families or more provide free common and grammar schools. Perry Miller and Thomas Johnson, two of the foremost scholars of Puritanism concluded "that in matters of education, the Puritans were leaders, not reactionaries, as resolute as they were sincere." [5]

The commitment of Thomas Jefferson and Benjamin Franklin to education is well known. But even more radical men of the Enlightenment, such as Thomas Paine, saw education as the primary means of creating and maintaining a democratic society. Harry Hayden Clark says, "The basic source of all Paine's hopes for a better world is his faith in education, the free play of reason, and enlightenment." [6]

Not only men of influence and scholarship believed in the virtue and efficacy of education; the working class did too. As early as the 1830s, radical workingmen

visualized education in its social and economic aspects as a major instrument of public policy. Nor was the role assigned to it in the society and the economy accidental. Skeptical of contemporary governments, and resolved to eliminate "aristocratic" influences from the economy, they proposed to employ education to destroy adventitious social distinctions and to ensure every man an equal opportunity for prosperity. They would educate to abolish class distinctions, to guarantee social and economic equality, and to preserve an open society in which merit would find its appropriate reward. [7]

    [5] P. Miller and T. Johnson (Eds.), *The Puritans: A Sourcebook of Their Writings*, pp. 695–700.
    [6] H. H. Clark (Ed.), *Thomas Paine, Key Writings*, pp. c–ci.
    [7] R. Welter, *Popular Education and Democratic Thought in America*, pp. 48–49.

26 The Illusion of Equality

Some of the most radical agitators of this period engaged in severe criticism of US society. But then instead of calling for revolution or even social legislation, they made the expansion of public education their major proposal.[8] The conservatives of the period had the same faith in education:

The leading Whigs virtually conceded by 1840 that government should be limited in scope and that its traditional positive functions should be assigned so far as possible to organized education. If enough of the people were well enough educated, their theory implied, the responsibilities of government would be very nearly fulfilled . . . Because they were conservatives, Whigs insisted upon the fullest possible provision for public education. Yet because they saw education in a democratic social context, they proposed to make it serve the widest possible range of public purpose.[9]

If we skip more than one hundred years and jump to 1954, we find that the school system was still the center of focus in attempts to actualize our commitment to democracy and equality. Surely it is no accident that civil rights groups such as the NAACP focused their efforts for racial equality on the education system. Moreover, their first success in challenging the "separate but equal" Jim Crow system was here. For in the realm of education our ideology, if not our actions, has always been clearest about the right of all for equality of opportunity. When civil-rights groups were able to make whites admit that separate was inherently unequal, the legal legitimacy of the old system had to be discarded.

Current battles for equality are still, for the most part, centered in the educational system. As in the past, the struggle is both internal and external. The internal debate centers on the role of clients within educational institutions. The debate takes a number of forms. The two most obvious are community control at the elementary and secondary level, and student participation in colleges and universities. In both cases, the essential issue is

8 Welter, p. 51.
9 Welter, p. 87.

the extent to which institutions should be controlled by a coalition of educational professionals and the traditional community and national establishments, versus the extent to which they should be controlled by the clients they directly serve. This issue is very complicated, and being an educational professional, I am undoubtedly biased. But even with that bias, it seems to me that this is in large measure another battle in the struggle for greater equality—this time for greater equality of power and authority within the educational system.

The external struggle focuses on who gets into the educational system and under what conditions. Because universal public education through high school is formally available to virtually everybody in our society, this debate centers on opportunities in higher education. Debate has continued over whether the federal government should try to make a college education available to all who desire it. The advocates of such a measure justify it in large measure on the need to provide greater equality of opportunity.

Campus disorders have generated criticism of the higher-education system. However, the focus of the backlash has been on control and discipline within the institutions of higher education. Few, if any, have advocated curtailment, much less abandonment, of higher education. Although we are increasingly dissatisfied with the way our schools and colleges have been operating, we still maintain our basic faith in the validity and efficacy of education. Over the long run, it seems likely that we will continue to move toward some form of universal higher education on a nationwide basis and that in large measure we will do this in the name of equality of opportunity.

Once again, we must make a concession to those who assign more importance to economic interest than ideological penchants. Our emphasis on schooling is, of course, intimately connected with the need of our economy for trained manpower. Much of our investment in education has been advocated quite explicitly as "good business." But this explanation alone is insufficient. Our strong emphasis on schooling is the result of the affinity between our economic requirements and our particular ideological values.

Part II will consider the question of equality of oppor-

tunity and higher education in some detail. At this point, however, I would like to summarize and focus the argument. Those
who feel they have a clear grasp of the line of argument may
wish to skip the next half-dozen paragraphs.

We have characterized American society as tired and
frustrated. We have suggested that this weariness and dissatisfaction is in part a result of our individual and collective preoccupation with endless striving. On the individual level, this
striving takes the form of expecting and working for a higher
level of income and an increasing number of commodities and
services. On the collective level, we call it economic growth or
even progress. The distinctive quality of this preoccupation is
precisely that it cannot be satisfied. Weariness results simply
because constant striving is tiring. Equally important, however,
striving has contributed to and aggravated social divisions and
conflicts. Whatever positive functions the social conflict of the
late 1960s and early 1970s may have had, it seems to have had a
wearing effect on our morale and energy. Most of all, however,
endless striving has been debilitating and frustrating because increasingly significant segments of our population find that the
goals for which they (or their parents) labored so hard were
hollow.

The concept of status inflation was introduced in an
attempt to clarify how our striving has become endless. Status
inflation is the social process through which the status value of
any absolute amount of individual resources decreases as the
average level of these resources increases. This inflationary
process makes our striving perpetual.

In order for status inflation to occur, individuals must
maintain an extraordinary concern about their own social status.
Americans are noted for such a preoccupation although at the
same time they show an unusual degree of egalitarianism toward
others.

A major source of this seemingly peculiar attitude toward
status is our strong emphasis on equality of opportunity. Equality
of opportunity, even if largely ideological, creates status insecurity. This insecurity results when both inequality and equality

of opportunity are present and people can lose status as well as gain it. This possibility of a drop in status or being surpassed by one's peers is a major cause of status insecurity and status seeking.

The strong emphasis on equality of opportunity in America has a complicated historical origin. Analytically, however, it can be understood as (1) a social mechanism which allows American society to maintain a dual emphasis on achievement and equality, and (2) the result of the interplay between these values and our long history of economic growth. Equality of opportunity means that everyone is created equal, but each is to be rewarded according to their individual achievements.

In a nutshell: weariness and frustration result from endless striving; endless striving is a result of status inflation and status seeking; status seeking is a result of the status insecurity which comes from our emphasis on equality of opportunity; and our emphasis on equality of opportunity is a result of economic development and our attempt to work out a compromise between the partially contradictory values of equality and achievement.

Now let me be more explicit in drawing the relationship between this analysis and the expansion of education. Formal education has had a central role in American society. Historically, we have had an almost irrepressible faith in education as a worthwhile end-in-itself and as a means of actualizing other social values. Attempts to maintain and increase equality of opportunity and expansion of our education facilities have gone hand in hand. Those committed to an egalitarian society have repeatedly tried to equalize the opportunities for education as the most effective means of overcoming entrenched privilege and inequality.

Liberal forces are generally still committed to such a strategy, and the current trend is to increase equality of opportunity by expanding the higher-education system. Until 1968 and the beginning of widespread student protest, opposition to such a program was limited to questioning the importance of education relative to other national priorities. Although some may have private reservations about increasing equality of opportunity, few if any take a public stand against this goal and fewer still question the effectiveness of expanded educational facilities.[10]

In my opinion, we need to question seriously both the traditional commitment to equality of opportunity and the expansion of higher education as a means of accomplishing it. The expansion of opportunities for higher education must be seen primarily as another round in our long history of status inflation. Those from lower-class and underprivileged backgrounds who receive a college education are likely (but by no means certain) to obtain a significantly higher status job and income than they would have obtained without higher education. But those from privileged backgrounds will retain their educational advantage by a variety of strategies: graduate degrees, postgraduate work, and attending prestigious institutions.

Consequently, the expansion of our higher education system may not produce either greater equality or equality of opportunity. Rather, the result may be more status inflation, more endless striving and more weariness and frustration.

Before proceeding to a detailed analysis of higher education and inequality, a comment is in order about the direction and extent of causation implied in the above argument. The kinds of relationships and linkages I have been describing (the relationship between weariness, endless striving and status inflation) are extremely complex. Moreover, some of the concepts like weariness and striving are imprecise if not vague. Consequently, I want to make clear that I am not arguing that each link in the chain causes the next step in the sense that it includes the necessary and sufficient conditions. An emphasis on equality of opportunity does not by itself cause status inflation. But *some* causation is suggested. Perhaps the appropriate wording is that each factor "contributes to the causation of" the next factor.

Finally, let me state the twofold purpose of the next part of the book. The first is to outline in some detail the reasons why an expansion of the higher-education system is not likely to

[10] There have, of course, been dissidents. Ivan Illich and Paul Goodman, for example, have long been skeptical of the value of schooling in general, at least in its traditional forms.

increase either equality or equality of opportunity significantly. This discussion is a prelude to Part III which attempts to state some of the consequences of educational expansion for social conflict in the United States. The second purpose is to illustrate why status inflation occurs in the educational system. Status inflation is a general phenomenon affecting many aspects of our society. The mechanisms which produce it will quite likely be different from those which operate in the educational sector. Nonetheless, a look at the more detailed relationships in this one limited sector seems both necessary and worthwhile.

Equality of Opportunity

Three

The expansion of the American educational system has usually been closely connected to some concept of increasing equality of opportunity, especially during the expansion of higher education since World War II. This goal is characteristic of policy statements by Democratic and Republican administrations and most "nonpartisan" groups interested in higher education.

Common Quest

The Carnegie Commission on Higher Education, headed by Clark Kerr, entitled their first major report *Quality and Equality* and stated on the first page: "What the American nation needs and expects from higher education in the critical years just ahead can be summed up in two phrases: quality of result and equality of access . . . The nation's campuses must act energetically and even aggressively to open up new channels to equality of educational opportunity."

In response to President Johnson's education message of February, 1968, the Department of Health, Education, and Welfare created an advisory panel which produced a report entitled *Toward a Long-Range Plan for Federal Financial Support for Higher Education*. To quote former HEW Secretary Wilbur Cohen's cover letter: [1] "The report concludes that federal aid to higher education in the future should emphasize two major national commitments: It should promote *equality of opportunity* by ensuring that all able students can afford to go on past secondary education, and that institutions are able to accommodate them. It should strengthen *graduate education and research*."

If anything, the public statements of the Nixon administration placed an even greater emphasis on equality of opportunity as the primary goal of its higher-education policy. President Nixon began his first higher-education message to Congress (March 19, 1970) with the following words:

No qualified student who wants to go to college should be barred by lack of money. That has long been a great American goal; I propose that we achieve it now. Something is basically unequal about opportunity for higher education when a young person whose family earns more than $15,000 a year is nine times more likely to attend college than a young person whose family earns less than $3,000. Something is basically wrong with federal policy toward higher education when it has failed to correct this inequity.

In terms of social science, equality of opportunity may be viewed as referring to certain patterns of social mobility. Social mobility may—but does not necessarily—influence the degree of inequality and opportunity. Therefore, the question

[1] US Department of Health, Education, and Welfare, *Toward a Long-Range Plan for Federal Financial Support to Higher Education.*

I wish to pose is how student admission and financial support will affect social mobility and whether such influences will have consequences for inequality and inequality of opportunity.

My thesis is twofold. First, while some forms of aid will have greater effects than others, none of the currently conceived types of aid is likely to produce significant changes in the degree of social class equality or equality of opportunity. Second, such aid may contribute significantly to equality and equality of opportunity for blacks. The following chapters will attempt to review the social theory and empirical evidence that lead to this conclusion.

However, we must first take care of a preliminary matter. The conclusion that student aid will have little effect on class differences but will affect racial differences is in part a result of the way certain concepts are defined. Consequently, we must spend several pages spelling out key definitions. For those who have a rudimentary grasp of the sociology of inequality, this section will be largely old hat, and they may wish to skip to the next section.

Definitions

The meaning of *inequality* is rather obvious; some individuals, organizations, communities, ethnic groups, and so on receive more of some valued resource (wealth, political power, education, and so on) than others. But if the meaning of inequality is relatively clear, a method of describing and measuring different degrees and types of inequality is much less clear. We can describe inequality in terms of an absolute reference point, for example, the number or percentage of those who make above six thousand dollars a year and those who make less than this. But such data in itself tells us little about the degree of inequality because the social meaning of six thousand dollars varies considerably from place to place and time to time.

Normally, social scientists try to measure inequality in terms of some type of frequency distribution. They ask, for example, how many people have incomes of less than two thousand dollars, how many from two thousand dollars to four thousand dollars, and so on. In the vast majority of civilized

societies, most people have low—frequently subsistence-level—
incomes. A small number have modest amounts of wealth and
income,[2] and a very small minority controls very large amounts
of the society's resources. In such societies, the shape of the
distribution of income, wealth, education, and so on, tends to
resemble a pyramid. But, of course, the shape of a distribution
may change over time or vary for different societies. In many
modern industrial societies, the shape of the distribution has
changed from a pyramid to a diamond. That is, supposedly
only a minority of the population has very low incomes, the
vast majority have middle-level incomes, and a small number
have very high incomes.

How best to measure such variations is a perennial
problem of social scientists. The most common technique is a
Lorenz curve. Essentially, this approach asks the question: What
percentage of the total income (or wealth, or years of schooling, and so on) of a society goes to a particular portion of the
population? For example, what percentage of the income goes
to the 10 per cent of the population who have the lowest incomes, or what percentage goes to the lowest 25 or 50 per cent?
Or we could ask what percentage of the income goes to the
next-to-lowest 10 per cent of the population, that is, those who
make more than the lowest 10 per cent of the population but
less than the other 80 per cent of the people. Or we could
consider the whole range of incomes and ask what percentage
of the total income goes to the lowest 10 per cent of the population, the second 10 per cent, the third, fourth, and so on. In
principle, we can refine this form of measurement to provide

[2] Wealth is the total amount of money and property *held* at *any
point in time*—irrespective of when these were acquired. Income is the
amount *received* during any *period* of time—usually a year—irrespective
of whether the things received were consumed, exchanged, or held. Although there are slight variations in the way economists define these
terms, the above meaning will be used throughout this book. While over
the long run there is necessarily a strong relationship between these two
variables, at any given point in time, it is quite possible that one of them
might be distributed considerably more equally than the other. As we
will see later, it seems likely that in the United States, income is now
distributed considerably more equally than wealth.

as much detail as we desire. We can ask what percentage of the income goes to the seventeenth percentile, to the fifty-sixth percentile, to the eighty-fifth, or even what proportion goes to each percentile from one through one hundred.

This form of measurement allows us to define meaningfully a society that is completely equal, a society that is completely unequal, or any degree of variation in between. Imagine a hypothetical society of one hundred people. If there were complete inequality, all of the income would go to one person, that is, 1 per cent of the population would receive 100 per cent of the income. If there was complete equality, the lowest 1 per cent (or the highest—or any other percentile since all are equal) would receive 1 per cent of the income.

All of the above discussion is background for one very simple and basic point. The concept of inequality deals with *relative* differences. Consequently, changes in the absolute level of resources does not necessarily have any effect on the degree or type of inequality. Inequality refers to the shape of the pyramid, not the absolute level of the pyramid. Consequently, the degree of inequality can be the same in a society that has an average annual per capita income of a hundred dollars as in one where it is ten thousand dollars. I would be embarrassed to belabor such an obvious point if the history of our country's ideology did not indicate that we have obscured this issue again and again. Our ideology frequently implies that economic growth automatically reduces inequality and increases social justice.

This misconception is, in turn, at least partly the basis of the similar confusion that surrounds the meaning of *opportunity*. Opportunity assumes some degree of inequality. In a society where everyone is equal—receives the same amount of income, education, and so on—opportunities are by definition equal. But, assuming unequal rewards, the concept of opportunity focuses on the question of whether some have a better chance (probability) to receive the higher rewards than others.

Inequality of opportunity can be conceptualized as a correlation between the statuses an individual has inherited (ascriptive status) and the statuses he has in some senses earned (achieved). To the extent that there is not perfect equality of opportunity, an individual's achieved statuses are in some degree influenced or determined by his ascribed statuses.[3] In this context, the ascriptive attributes are the socioeconomic characteristics or statuses (SES) of the individual's parents (for example, their education, occupation, or income) while the achieved statuses are the individual's own education, occupation, and income.

No necessary relationship exists between the degree of inequality and the degree of inequality of opportunity. (The exception is the limiting cases of perfect equality, where there is necessarily perfect equality of opportunity.) Complete equality of opportunity is logically possible within a stratification system that has a high degree of inequality, for example, a tall narrow pyramid. Inversely, systems with a low degree of inequality can logically be rigid caste systems with the children automatically receiving the status of their parents. Actually, societies with high degrees of inequality do in practice tend to have a low degree of equality of opportunity. The precise strength and nature of the empirical relationship is determined by the rates and types of social mobility.

Social mobility refers to upward and downward changes in the status of individuals or families.[4] We are concerned primarily with intergenerational changes: parents compared with their children. As with inequality, intergenerational mobility

[3] Perfect equality of opportunity means that for the population as a whole, there is no statistical correlation between ascribed and achieved statuses. Just as the degree of inequality is measured by the extent of departure from a straight Lorenz curve, the degree of equality of opportunity is measured by the extent to which the correlation between ascribed statuses and achieved statuses approaches the model of statistical independence. No existing society comes close to having reached these perfect models. It is pointless, however, to talk about increasing equality of opportunity unless we mean more closely approximating such models. As we shall see shortly, increasing the level of income, or the amount of upward mobility may or may not affect equality of opportunity.

[4] Horizontal movement is also possible, but here we are concerned only with vertical mobility. It is also possible for various kinds of collectivities to experience mobility, but our unit of measurement at this point is the individual.

can be measured either in absolute or in relative terms. A son may be upwardly mobile in absolute terms because his annual income averages six thousand dollars over his lifetime compared with his father's average of five thousand dollars. But he may at the same time be downwardly mobile in relative terms if five thousand dollars fell above the national average during most of the father's career while six thousand dollars fell below the national average during most of the son's working career.

There is a general principle which governs the pattern of intergenerational mobility necessary for equality of opportunity: the adult members of each class or stratum must be composed of members who, with respect to their social origins, are proportionately representative of each class or stratum in the society. For purposes of example, assume a society with three classes: an upper, middle, and lower class with 10, 30, and 60 per cent of the population, respectively. For there to be equality of opportunity, in the next generation, 60 per cent of the upper class would have to come from lower-class origins, 30 per cent from middle-class origins, and only 10 per cent from upper-class origins. Likewise, the middle and lower class must also recruit their members in the same proportions: 10 per cent from the upper, 30 per cent from the middle, and 60 per cent from the lower.

The actual amount of upward and downward mobility required to actualize the above principle depends upon (1) the initial degree of inequality, (2) changes in the degree of inequality and level of wealth during a given generation, and (3) demographic factors. That is, it depends upon the initial shape of the pyramid (distribution), changes in the level and shape of the pyramid, and the initial socioeconomic composition of the younger generation. Let us begin with the case where all of the above factors are constant and then consider more complex situations where one or more of these factors changes. If all of these factors are constant, perfect equality of opportunity can occur only if upward and downward mobility are equal in absolute terms and inversely proportionate in relative terms.

For purposes of illustration, let us imagine a hypothetical

society of five-hundred families. Each family consists of a husband, wife, and two children. This society is divided into two distinct social classes: one hundred of the families (200 adults) are in the upper class (20 per cent) and four hundred (800 adults) are in the lower class (80 per cent). For the moment, let us also assume that for the next fifty years, the level and distribution of income (and occupations, education, and so on) remain constant.

In such a society, perfect equality of opportunity requires that 80 per cent of the upper class in the next generation must be recruited from the lower class, while only 20 per cent of the new upper class would be children of upper-class parents. In absolute terms, the upper class in the next generation would be made up of 160 individuals of lower-class parents and forty individuals of upper-class parents. In a similar manner, 20 per cent of the lower class in the next generation would need to come from the upper class and 80 per cent from the lower class. In absolute terms, 160 persons would be of upper-class origins while 640 persons would be of lower-class origins. We see that the absolute level of upward and downward mobility are equal: 160 uppers moved down and 160 lowers moved up. But the first 160 represents 80 per cent of those of upper-class origin, while the second 160 represents only 20 per cent of those with lower-class origins. Hence, the relative rates of mobility are inversely proportionate. Under these conditions, each individual has an equal life chance with every other person. Everyone has a two-in-ten chance of being in the upper class when he or she is an adult and inversely all have a eight-in-ten chance of being in the lower class.

If the degree of inequality were different, the absolute and proportionate amounts of mobility required for equality of opportunity would vary. Assume a second hypothetical society exactly like the first except that the upper class included only 50 families (100 adults) and the lower class included 450 families (900 adults). In this situation, equality of opportunity would require that 90 move up and 90 move down. Proportionately, the latter 90 individuals would constitute 10 per cent of the lower class children while the former 90 individuals would constitute 90 per cent of the upper-class children. In this society, each child would have a one-in-ten chance of becoming an adult member of the upper class and conversely a nine-in-ten chance of winding up in the lower class. The comparison of these two hypothetical societies illustrates how variations in the degree of inequality affects the patterns of mobility required for equality of opportunity.

Up to this point, we have assumed that the level of the pyramid (distribution) was constant: that there were no changes in the level of economic development. Of course, this is not the case in modern industrial societies. Because of economic growth, the absolute level of the pyramid tends to shift upward. For example, between 1947 and 1967—approximately one generation—the average family income in the United States increased from approximately $4500 to $8000 (in constant dollars controlled for inflation). This was a 176 per cent increase.[5] This means that upper-class children can loose social status in relative terms without reducing their absolute level of living. In our hypothetical society, this would mean that the 160 upper-class children who became lower-class adults would still have approximately the same standard of living that they experienced growing up, but that 160 members of the lower class had passed them up. Because the line which divides the uppers from the lowers is moving up, these 160 whose parents were upper class have become members of the lower class, while the 160 from lower-class backgrounds would not only be much better off absolutely, but they would have crossed the line into the upper class. Supposedly, a pattern such as this would soften some of the deprivation that the children of the upper class would feel from their relative downward mobility.

In addition to changes in the level of economic development, there can be changes in the shape of the pyramid (distribution) which will, of course, affect the patterns of mobility required for perfect equality of opportunity. If the society is becoming more equal, the absolute level of upward mobility

[5] U. S. Bureau of the Census, "Income in 1967 of Families in the United States," *Current Population Reports*, P-60(190), p. 22.

may exceed the absolute level of downward mobility, though the relative rates will still be inversely proportional. If our hypothetical society changed over the course of a generation so that 40 per cent of the population were in the upper class and 60 per cent were in the lower class—instead of 20 per cent and 80 per cent—320 people would have to move up while 120 would have to move down in order to have equality of opportunity. This 320 would constitute 40 per cent of the lower class while the 120 would constitute 60 per cent of the upper class, but the children from both classes would have a four-in-ten chance of becoming upper class and a six-in-ten chance of becoming lower class. If the society became more unequal, the opposite pattern would be necessary and the absolute level of downward mobility would have to exceed the level of upward mobility.[6]

There is another important factor which may influence the rates of mobility required for equality of opportunity. Up to this point, we have assumed that each social class furnished (through reproduction) the same percentage of the new generation that it made up of the old generation. That is, we assumed that upper-class couples had 20 per cent of the children and lower-class couples had 80 per cent of the children. In reality, the lower classes usually have higher birth rates than the upper classes so the latter produce a smaller proportion of the new generation than they constituted of the older generation. If the degree of inequality stays the same (or decreases), this means that there is "extra" room at the top which needs to be filled by children of lower-class parents. Back to our hypothetical society: Let us assume that out of the thousand children produced, nine hundred are from lower-class families and one hundred are from upper-class families. This means that if the

[6] Logically and methodologically, changes in the degree of inequality over time involve the same relationships as the comparison of two different societies with varying degrees of inequality. Sociologically there are, of course, important differences in variations between societies at a given point in time and changes in a single society over time. Consequently, I have given separate examples of each case, though the examples are interchangeable from a methodological point of view.

degree of inequality is to stay the same—200 upper-class adults
and 800 lower-class adults—one hundred of the lower-class children are going to have to move into the upper class simply
because this class has failed to reproduce itself. If both the
existing degree of inequality and equality of opportunity are
maintained, 180 lower class children will move up and 80 upper-
class children will move down. As in the other instances, the
rates of mobility are inversely proportionate: 80 per cent of
the upper class moves down and 20 per cent of the lower class
moves up.

Up to this point, we have talked as if the shape of the
distribution set the limits for the types of mobility that could
occur. This has been a heuristic device, however, to aid in explaining the relationship between mobility and opportunity.
Empirically, the connections are quite the opposite. In most
societies, the shape of the stratification structure is largely a
result of the past patterns of mobility. The shape remains constant if upward movement just matches downward movement
in absolute terms. The shape changes to the extent that this
condition is not met.

This rather long tangent on different patterns of mobility is to make one simple point: the rates and amount of
upward and downward mobility do not by themselves tell you
anything about equality of opportunity. Mobility must be interpreted in relationship to the initial degree of inequality,
changes in inequality, changes in the absolute level of welfare,
and demographic factors like differential birth and death rates
in order to measure the degree of equality of opportunity.

Several subpoints are worth stressing. First, even if a
very high proportion of those in the upper class come from
lower class backgrounds, there is not necessarily equality of
opportunity. In our hypothetical society, even if 60 per cent
of the upper class came from lower-class origins—a phenomenally high rate of inflow—upper-class children would still have
a great advantage. More specifically, upper-class children would
have a four-in-ten chance of becoming upper-class adults,
while lower-class children would have one-and-a-half-in-ten-
chance of becoming upper-class adults. The other side of this

coin is the second point: equality of opportunity requires phenomenally high rates of downward mobility for the upper classes—at least when there is significant inequality in the society. Third, and most important, the rate of upward mobility of those on the bottom in absolute terms does *not* necessarily have any effect on either inequality or opportunity. For example, in the United States, a great majority of sons will be upwardly mobile in the sense that they will have more education and a higher income than their fathers, simply because the average level of education and income are increasing dramatically. However, the crucial question that the concept of equality of opportunity raises is not whether sons are better educated than their fathers, *but whether the sons of poorly educated fathers have less education (or occupational status, or wealth) than the sons of well educated fathers.* As Burton Clark notes, there is an important distinction between raising the average level of education or increasing the number of individuals who enter college and equalizing the educational attainment of those with equal ability without regard to irrelevant criteria such as socioeconomic status, race, or place of residence.[7] If the increases of the lower class are matched by the increases of the upper class, existing structures of inequality and inequality of opportunity remain unchanged.

In short, (1) welfare (income, education, and so on), (2) inequality, (3) opportunity, and (4) mobility are all distinct social attributes related to different social processes. Changes in one do not necessarily mean changes in the others.

---

[7] B. Clark, *Educating the Expert Society*, p. 77.

Social Class I

Four

The next two chapters will focus on the way social class [1] differences—primarily variations in parents' education, occupation, and income—influence opportunities for higher education and how these opportunities will in turn affect the structure of inequality. For the moment, we will ignore the effects of race because this matter will be considered in detail in a later chapter. Let us now sketch out the general line of argument.

Pushing on a Limber Rod

The chain of causation linking college admission and financial-aid policies with inequality and inequality of oppor-

---

[1] "Social class" is used here in a broad sense, rather than in the restricted Marxian sense. The term social strata would be technically more correct, but it is stylistically awkward and obscure in meaning to those not initiated into the mysteries of the social stratification literature. The literature on this issue is very large, but for a short discussion of the issue see A. M. Rose, "The Concept of Class in American Sociology," *Social Research*, 1958, 25, 53–69.

tunity in the social stratification system is long and complex. Taken by itself, any one of the links involves fairly strong relationships (for example, the relation between the availability of student aid and lower-class enrollment in college or between educational attainment and occupational attainment). But taken as a whole, inputs on one end of the chain have only modest effects at the other end. Student aid may have a significant effect on equalizing opportunities for college education, but its effect on equalizing occupational attainment will be considerably weaker and the effect on equalizing income and wealth weaker yet.

Consequently, attempting to affect the structure of economic inequality through student aid at the college level is analogous to trying to move a heavy rock situated some distance away by pushing on it with a series of short sticks tied together to form a long rod. Although each stick may be quite strong, and two sticks tied end to end may provide a sturdy pole, a long series of such sticks is an ineffectual tool.

Now let me present the argument in more technical terms. (Those without a background in statistics will want to skip over the next two paragraphs. They will have missed nothing central to the main argument.) Although many of the linkages are significant, available data do not indicate that any factor accounts for more than about 60 per cent of the variance in the next factor in the chain. In most cases, the strength of the relationship is much weaker. For example, a recent analysis of project TALENT data correlated thirty-eight personal and environmental factors with college attendance.[2] The multiple correlation coefficients for all thirty-eight variables was .674 for males and .733 for females. For males, only five factors had a zero-order correlation of .30 or more (the highest being .549). The partial coefficients were of course much lower. The coefficients for the females were in some cases slightly higher. When these coefficients are squared, we see that any causal connections which exist are at best "loose." Although other studies have sometimes found stronger relationships be-

[2] J. K. Folger, H. S. Astin, and A. E. Bayer, *Human Resources and Higher Education.*

tween similar sets of variables, these figures are not unrepresentative.

A hypothethical example may help to clarify this line of argument. Let us assume a causal model involving five variables linked in sequence. Further, assume that each linkage is a linear relationship with a regression coefficient of .50. Student aid counteracts the effects of parents' SES, parents' SES influences educational attainment, educational attainment influences occupational attainment, occupational attainment influences income, income influences wealth. In such a model, the coefficient for the effect of multiple links is equal to the product of the individual coefficients. For example, the regression coefficient linking aid and education is the product of the coefficient linking aid and SES (.50), .50 $\times$ .50 = .25. The coefficient linking aid and wealth is .03125, that is, .50 $\times$ .50 $\times$ .50 $\times$ .50 $\times$ .50. This means, for example, that if the financial resources available for college *were completely equalized,* the distribution of wealth would be 3.1 per cent more equal. (That is, the area under the Lorenz curve would be 3.1 per cent larger.) Of course, a 3.1 per cent change in the distribution of wealth is not insignificant although it is small. But even this small change in the distribution of wealth was attained under what are probably unduly optimistic assumptions, namely, that resources available to attend college are completely equal and that the coefficients are .50. Even if the coefficients were raised to .60, equality of wealth would be affected by about 5 per cent, while coefficients of .70—which are totally unrealistic—would equalize things about 11 per cent. Consequently, even relatively large inputs at one end of the chain are largely diluted, if not washed out, when their effects reach the other end.[3]

My conclusions about the probable effects of aid on in-

[3] The model suggested above is intended only to illustrate the "wash-out effect," and not to portray the actual causal relations. For example, a path analysis would undoubtedly show that parents' SES has a direct effect on children's occupational attainment, in addition to an indirect effect through the child's level of education. The coefficients used in the illustration are, however, large enough to include both direct and indirect effects for virtually all of the possible relationships.

equality are at variance with other analyses for two reasons. First, other studies oriented toward higher-education policy have tended to look primarily at short-run effects (or more accurately, next-link effects), for example, how many additional lower-class young people enroll in college as a result of increased financial aid, rather than the more distant consequences such as intergenerational mobility and the distribution of wealth. The second, less important factor concerns how the variables used to measure inequality and opportunity are conceptualized. In past studies, variables have often necessarily been conceptualized in an imprecise manner. For example, the level of educational attainment is often measured in terms of the number of years of school completed. Such a method makes four years at Podunck College with a major in physical education and a C average equal to four years at MIT with a degree in electrical engineering and an A average. But an individual with the latter training is likely to have a significantly different life experience than the one with the former. My conceptualizations and measurements are no better, but I have tried to be sensitive to the probable consequences of such inaccuracies in measurement and to take them into account in drawing conclusions.

The discussion is presented in the order of causal sequence through which student aid would presumably operate. First, we focus on the current state of inequality of opportunity, that is, the effect of socioeconomic status on the college student. Second, we analyze the consequences of financial aid, tuition reduction, and income-tax credits on relatively short-term changes, for example, enrollment rates by SES categories. In this connection, we discuss the efficacy of the alternative forms of aid on these short-term consequences. Finally, we consider how these two sets of phenomena—the drag of SES and the push of publicly financed schooling—have interacted and influenced the stratification system in the past.

The first task is to review the nature of the inequalities of opportunity that currently exist within the American higher-education system. More specifically, let us see how SES influences: (1) college attendance, (2) progress in college, (3) the type and quality of the college attended, (4) the relationship

48   The Illusion of Equality

of career choices to the college major, (5) enrollment and progress in graduate school, and (6) occupational attainment after graduate school.

SES and Initial Enrollment

There has never been much question in the past about whether SES affects one's chances of attending college; clearly those from upper SES groups were more likely to enroll. This is still true. Information from the Bureau of the Census for 1968 reveals how college enrollment rates varied by level of income for families with dependents between eighteen and twenty-four years. Sixteen per cent of the families earning less than three thousand dollars a year had children enrolled in college. The percentage steadily increased with income; 63 per cent of the families making fifteen thousand dollars a year or more had children in college.[4] The educational level of the head of the household has a similar effect. About 35 per cent of the children who come from families whose head has less than an eighth-grade education manage to enroll in college. In contrast, 88 per cent of those from families headed by a college graduate will attend college.[5]

The above figures significantly understate the effect of socioeconomic background on educational attainment because they only tell us what happens to those who have already managed to complete high school. But individuals of low SES are also much less likely to complete high school than are individuals of high SES. Although aid to college students cannot be expected to alleviate inequalities at lower levels in the school

[4] These figures understate the effect of income because they show the percentage of families which have at least one child in college. However, low-income families tend to have more children than high-income families and rarely have more than one child in college at the same time. Therefore, these figures regard the lower-income family with one of its three college-age children in college as having the same "opportunity" as the upper-income family with both of its two children enrolled in college.
[5] US Bureau of the Census, "School Enrollment: October 1968 and 1967," *Current Population Reports*, P-20 (190).

system, the full life-time effect of SES on one's chances of attending college must be kept in mind.

It could be argued that upper-SES groups have higher enrollment rates not because of the advantage of their class background but because they are smarter. However, when both SES and intellectual ability of high school graduates are measured and compared with college enrollment rates we see that differences in ability do not fully explain the effects of SES. In 1962, Project TALENT did a follow-up study of a national sample of students who were first tested in the eleventh grade in 1960. They found that when ability and sex are controlled, SES still has a significant influence on a person's chances of attending college. The individuals were classified according to SES and ability quartiles. For those in the same ability quartile, the top SES groups tended to have an enrollment rate at least 30 per cent and sometimes 40 per cent higher than the lowest SES groups. For example, 61 per cent of the males in the top ability quartile and the lowest SES quartile enrolled in college, compared with 92 per cent for high-SES males in the same ability quartile. For women, the effect of SES was even stronger. Forty-two per cent of the high-ability low-SES women enrolled in college, while 87 per cent of those with the same ability, but high SES enrolled. The effect of SES is even stronger for the third (next-to-the-highest) ability quartile. In this ability group, high-SES individuals, both men and women, were about two-and-a-half times more likely to attend college than those with the same ability but from the lowest SES quartile.[6] Although the details of other studies vary slightly, the basic picture is the same.[7] Moreover, these findings understate the effect of SES since the measures of ability are probably

[6] Project TALENT, *One Year Follow-up Study, Cooperative Research Project No. 2333*, Pittsburgh: University of Pittsburgh, School of Education, 1966.

[7] See, for example, W. H. Sewell and V. P. Shah, "Socioeconomic Status, Intelligence, and the Attainment of Higher Education," *Sociology of Education*, 40 (Winter 1967), 1–23; Folger, Astin, and Bayer, *Human Resources and Higher Education;* and R. F. Berdie, *Decisions for Tomorrow, Plans of High School Seniors.*

in some degree biased in favor of the higher SES individuals.

In summary, SES has a definite impact on an individual's chances of attending college whether SES is measured in terms of income, occupation or education. The relationship holds even when ability and a wide variety of other factors are controlled. Its effect is less for those of high ability and for males. However, even for men in the top ability quartile, the data available show a 30 per cent differential in the college-attendance rates of high school graduates between the bottom and top SES quartile. Now let us turn to the question of whether SES continues to affect academic achievement after the initial barrier of college enrollment has been overcome.

SES and Progress in College

An individual's socioeconomic background influences not only his chances of entering college, but also his chances of staying in school and completing his degree. A classic study of the early 1950s claimed that after students had enrolled in college, their progress was little affected by SES and was determined primarily by ability. Later studies seem to indicate that although the effect of family background is weaker, it continues to play a significant role in the individual's likelihood of completing college.[8] A study which did an eight year follow-up of Wisconsin high school graduates found that boys from high-SES families are almost twice as likely to graduate as those with low SES and upper-class girls have about a 50 per cent better chance than lower-class girls. Even when differences in intellectual ability are taken into account, much of the difference remains. For example, in the Wisconsin study, 71 per cent of the high-ability males from the top SES quartile graduated from college while only 38 per cent of those with the same ability level, but from the low SES quartile, completed college.[9] My own analysis of 1968 data collected by the Bureau of the Census indicates an even stronger relationship for high school graduates

[8] Compare D. L. Wolfle, "Educational Opportunity, Measured Intelligence, and Social Background," p. 232, with Folger, Astin, and Bayer, pp. 316–321.
[9] Sewell and Shah.

under 35 years of age—although this data may be biased. For example, those who came from families headed by a college graduate were three times as likely to complete college as those from families headed by a high school graduate and five times as likely to graduate as those from families whose head had an eighth-grade education.[10]

In short, SES continues to influence educational attainment for those who have entered college although its effects are weaker at this point than on initial enrollment. Even when ability is controlled, graduation rates run from 20 to 60 per cent higher for those from the top SES categories than for those from the bottom ones.

SES and Type of College

The type and status of the college attended are important to us for at least two reasons. First, the quality and prestige of a college affects later occupational attainment or, at the very least, chances of enrolling in a graduate school.

Second, colleges which have high admission standards— and usually high prestige—have much lower attrition rates than the less selective institutions. Therefore, if SES is related to the type of college attended, SES necessarily influences the chances of completing college—one of the findings in the preceding section. We will now explore this influence and later examine how the type of college affects occupational attainment.

Socioeconomic status is definitely related to the type and selectivity of the college attended, even when differences in ability are taken into account. For example, data from the Project TALENT study indicate that those in the top ability quartile and the lowest SES quartile are five times more likely to attend junior colleges than students of the same ability who are in the highest SES quartile.[11] The effect of SES is less for the lower ability groups but is still substantial.

The nature of the institution—junior college, four-year

[10] M. Milner, Jr., "The Effects of Federal Aid to Higher Education on Social Inequality," p. 48.
[11] Milner, p. 53.

college, or university—also clearly affects the quality of the student body. For example, in 1969, 10 per cent of the freshmen who enrolled in junior colleges had high school averages of B+ or above. The figure was 36 per cent for four-year colleges and 40 per cent for universities. By this measure, universities were four times more selective than junior colleges.[12]

The selectivity (or student-body ability level) is in turn connected with graduation rates. For example, a follow-up of students five years after they entered a college showed that approximately 50 per cent of the men who attended low selectivity four-year colleges completed their degrees. By way of comparison, the completion rate was between 60 and 75 per cent for high-selectivity colleges. The most dramatic finding, however, was that only 20 per cent of those who entered junior colleges completed their degrees. For women, the effect of selectivity was slightly less within four-year colleges, but the gap between junior colleges and four-year colleges was about the same.[13]

In summary, low-SES students tend to enroll in the poorer quality colleges—although there are many exceptions— and this significantly reduces their chances of completing a college degree. In order to grasp the full significance of such enrollments, let us keep in mind that the future expansion of college enrollments is expected primarily in the traditionally lower quality two-year colleges. Paradoxically, the expansion of opportunities to enroll in college may actually increase the gap in completion rates between the low and high socioeconomic groups.

Earlier, we noted that the type of college one attends also affects occupational status and income. For a long time, it has been common knowledge that it is advantageous to attend

[12] American Council on Education, *National Norms for Entering College Freshmen—Fall, 1969*, p. 35. The selectivity ratio depends in part on the cutting point selected. For example, if an A or A+ were the criterion, universities would be seven times as selective as junior colleges. If a B average were the cutting point, universities would be a little over twice as selective.

[13] Folger, Astin, and Bayer, p. 173.

a "good" college.[14] A study of nine thousand college graduates conducted in 1947 found a definite correlation between salary and the type of college attended.[15] For example, graduates of Harvard, Yale, and Princeton had an average income in 1947 of $7,356 while other Ivy League graduates averaged $6,142. The differences were even greater for other types of schools: MIT—$5,382, twenty famous eastern colleges—$5,287, Big Ten schools—$5,176, all other Midwestern colleges—$4,322, all other Eastern colleges—$4,235.

A Bureau of the Census study conducted in 1967 confirms the 1947 findings.[16] Colleges were ranked on the basis of the average aptitude of entering freshmen. The relationship between the rank of colleges and 1966 median earnings was clear. For example, those with a bachelor's degree from a low ranked institution had a median income of $7,881, whereas the figures were $9,752 and $11,678 for medium and high institutions respectively.

The effect is especially strong at the bachelor's-degree level where those attending low ranking colleges make 33 per cent less on the average than those from top ranked institutions. This relationship is especially significant because much of the expansion in enrollment is occurring in the institutions with a relatively low ranking.

SES, Major, and Career Choice

Another way in which a person's class background influences his future class position is through the selection of a college major and its subsequent effect on his occupation. A nationwide study of 1958 college graduates found that 32 per

[14] The connection between the status of the college attended and income is in part spurious. Traditionally, the sons of well-to-do families have gone to high prestige schools, but in most cases these individuals would have had high incomes no matter what college they attended! Second, insofar as the relationship is not spurious, a number of possible intervening factors are involved, namely, whether the advantage is due to better training, personal contacts, the prestigious degree, and so on.

[15] See B. Clark, *Educating the Expert Society*, p. 73.

[16] US Bureau of the Census, "Men with College Degrees: March 1967," *Current Population Reports*, P-20 (180).

cent of those graduates who were premedical majors had fathers
who were classified as professionals, although only 11 per cent
of the total graduating class had fathers with this occupational
designation. By way of contrast, 23 per cent of the fathers were
classified as farmers, farm laborers, or service workers. Yet
their sons made up 41 per cent of those who majored in education.[17] Medicine is, of course, ranked among occupations of
the highest status whereas primary or secondary teaching has
traditionally been a relatively low-status occupation for college
educated men. Several sophisticated analyses of the effects of
SES on career choice have found that a relationship exists—
though it is complicated—even when the effects of ability are
taken into account. Exactly why students from low-SES backgrounds are more likely to choose low-status occupations than
high-status ones is not fully understood. Apparently, lack of
money for extended training, different sets of values and motivations, and the tendency of sons to select the occupation of their
fathers all play a role. Moreover, as students proceed through
their college careers, these factors apparently become stronger
and students tend to change into fields dominated by students
whose backgrounds are similar to their own.[18]

SES and Graduate Education

Although the effect of socioeconomic background on
the chances of enrolling in graduate school is less than its effect
on earlier steps in higher education, there is nonetheless a measurable impact. One study found that if ability was held constant, those in the highest socioeconomic quartile were almost
twice as likely to enroll in graduate school in the first year
after college graduation as those from the lowest socioeconomic

[17] L. Sharp, *Two Years After the College Degree*, Table A4M.
[18] See J. Davis, *Career Decisions*; J. Davis, "The Campus as a Frog
Pond: An Application of the Theory of Relative Deprivation to the
Career Decisions of College Men," *American Journal of Sociology*, 1966,
72, 17–31; C. E. Werts, "Social Class and Initial Career Choice of College
Freshmen," *Sociology of Education*, 1966, *39*, 348–358; C. E. Werts, "Career Changes in College," *Sociology of Education*, 1967, *40*, 90–95; and
C. E. Werts, "Path Analysis: Testimony of a Proselyte," *American Jour-
nal of Sociology*, 1968, *73*, 509–512.

quartile. For example, 54 per cent of those in the highest ability and the highest SES group enrolled in graduate school whereas 30 per cent of those in the same ability group but with low SES enrolled. These figures probably overstate the effect of SES because many lower-SES students enroll in graduate school in later years. However, it is unlikely that this later enrollment eliminates the disparity. Several studies have indicated that the effect of SES is considerably less for women. In fact, low-SES women sometimes enroll in graduate school more frequently than women from upper-class backgrounds.[19]

SES apparently also influences the choice of graduate school both directly and by its influence on the selection of the undergraduate school. One study found that family income influenced selection of a graduate school more than ability.[20] In sum, SES probably continues to have some effect on who enrolls in graduate school, who completes graduate degrees, and whether one attends a high- or low-status institution. The effects at this stage are admittedly much smaller than at earlier points in the educational system, but they are not insignificant in affecting equality of opportunity.

SES and Achievement After Higher Education

The entire preceding discussion has been based on the obvious fact that one of the primary ways class background influences achievement is by its effect on the education received. But we must not forget that socioeconomic background affects later achievement (and consequently later SES) through channels other than education. The inheritance of wealth (or the failure to inherit it!) is the most obvious mechanism, but there are many others.

[19] See US Department of Health, Education, and Welfare, *Toward a Long-Range Plan for Federal Financial Support for Higher Education*. For additional data, much of which show SES to have a somewhat weaker effect, see E. L. Wegner, "Some Factors in Obtaining Postgraduate Education," *Sociology of Education*, 1969, *42*, 154–169; J. Davis, *Great Aspirations*, p. 118; Sharp; Folger, Astin, and Bayer; and J. L. Spaeth, "The Allocation of College Graduates to Graduate and Professional Schools," *Sociology of Education*, 1968, *41*, 342–349.
[20] Spaeth.

The most extensive study to date of achievement in the occupational structure found that the effect of education on the status of one's first job was only twice as great as the *direct* effect of the occupational status of one's father.[21] This direct impact is in addition to the influence of the father's occupation on the son's level of education. The direct influence of the father's occupation decreases, relative to the effect of the son's own level of education, for later stages in the son's career pattern, but it by no means disappears. This study deals with men at all levels of the educational and occupational structure, so it might be argued that the influence of family background disappears for those who have completed the highest levels of education and are working in professional occupations. However, evidence indicates that class origin affects the later occupational achievements even of those who have received doctoral degrees.[22]

The essential point to grasp is that even total and complete equality of opportunity at all levels of the educational system—a very unlikely prospect—will not eliminate the advantages (or disadvantages) of different socioeconomic backgrounds.

In this chapter, we have focused upon the effects of socioeconomic background on the individual's college career. The general findings are obvious: At a variety of points, individuals from high-SES backgrounds have a definite advantage over those from low-SES backgrounds. More specifically, high-SES individuals are more likely to (1) enroll in college, (2) stay there and graduate, (3) attend a high quality institution, (4) major in a subject that leads to a high-status occupation, (5) enroll

[21] P. Blau and O. D. Duncan, *The American Occupational Structure*, p. 170.

[22] D. Crane, "Scientists at Major and Minor Universities," *American Sociological Review*, 1965, *30*, 699–714; and D. Crane, "Social Class Origin and Academic Success: The Influence of Two Stratification Systems on Academic Careers," *Sociology of Education*, 1969, *42*, 1–17; L. L. Hargens and W. O. Hagstrom, "Sponsored and Contest Mobility of American Academic Scientists," *Sociology of Education*, 1967, *40*, 24–38; L. L. Hargens, "Patterns of Mobility of New PhD's Among American Academic Institutions," *Sociology of Education*, 1969, *42*, 18–37.

in graduate school and obtain a graduate degree, and (6) perform well and advance further in their chosen occupation. A related finding, which is hardly surprising, is that the effect of SES seems to weaken the further an individual has progressed through the higher-education system. The most plausible interpretation is that as individuals mature, the status and social relationships of their family of origin make up a decreasing part of their total set of social relationships. At the same time, more recently acquired relationships—especially academically achieved statuses—play an important role in shaping their personality structure and behavior and especially their academic performance. However, it is at least mildly surprising that socioeconomic background apparently continues to affect the academic and occupational achievement not only of graduate students but even those who have obtained Ph.D. degrees from high-prestige institutions.

Of course, we would expect that SES would have some effect; but the important question concerns its strength or significance. The answer to this question is in large measure dependent upon the reference point. Compared with most other societies, present and past, a high degree of egalitarianism exists in this country and the effect of ascribed status is very modest—generally less than measured ability. When considered in terms of causation (or "variance accounted for"), the effects of SES are quite significant but modest. However, when we compare the findings to some model of perfect equality or perfect equality of opportunity, we see that the effects of SES are very great. It can hardly be argued that the educational system is truly egalitarian when those from the upper SES quartile are up to three times more likely to enter college than those with the same level of ability from the lower quartile. And we must keep in mind that measures of ability are probably biased in favor of those from high-socioeconomic backgrounds and that actual inequities are greater than the data indicate.

Regardless of which of these perspectives is used to interpret the data, one implication of these findings is clear: simply reducing the inequality of opportunity at the point of entry into college—or even throughout the undergraduate career—cannot be expected to equalize fully the life chances of those from various socioeconomic backgrounds. Whether it will make a significant contribution toward reducing inequality and inequality of opportunity in the societal stratification system is a question we will consider in subsequent chapters. Next, however, we must consider the extent to which expanded student aid will equalize access to the higher-education system.

Social Class II

Five

We have seen that at every point in the process of attaining a higher education, socioeconomic background seems to exert influence in producing inequality of opportunity. These findings are hardly startling, but they help to set the context for our next problem: Can these inequalities be removed or even significantly reduced by financial aid to students?

Before we attempt to answer this question in even a preliminary way, the meaning of financial aid must be specified. Normally, the term is used to refer to scholarships (grants), loans, and work-study programs which help students meet the cost of attending college. This discussion will broaden the normal usage of this term to include two other methods of helping students pay for a college education: tax relief to students or their parents (or both), and subsidized services which are usually reflected in lower tuition. The second of these devices is the most common form of financial aid to students, and most students receive some assistance. Few colleges are profit-making enterprises, and most spend more on their students than they receive in tuition and fees. This financial situation is, of course, especially true for institutions which are supported by state and local governments and whose tuition is, relatively speaking, low. The extension of lowered tuition by federal grants to colleges and universities is frequently advocated. The first mechanism, tax relief, has not been widely used but has been frequently proposed since the early 1960s. This proposal would allow persons paying for a college education—usually parents—to deduct some portion of these costs from their income-tax liabilities. There may be other means of assisting students and their families to cover the cost of higher education, but grants, loans, work-study, lowered tuition, and tax relief are the five most widely discussed alternatives.

Impact of Aid

Now to return to the question: Can inequalities in our society be reduced by financial aid to students? Expanded aid will probably help some, but not very much. There is a surprising amount of agreement on this conclusion—the frequent political rhetoric to the contrary notwithstanding. Christopher Jencks and David Riesman in their widely discussed book, *The Academic Revolution,* conclude: "All in all, then, we are inclined to be skeptical about theories that emphasize the high cost of attending college as the major obstacle and to look for other explanations of the obvious relationship between class background and attainment." [1] A review of the literature on the effects of financial aid to students (which includes some twenty items of research covering about the same number of years) reaches a similar conclusion: "The relation between finances and college attendance is a complex one. Although money emerges as an important factor, it has come to be generally accepted that grant aid alone, offered at the end of the senior year of high school, will have relatively little effect on increasing the number and proportion of students who will attend

[1] Jencks and Riesman, p. 21.

college." [2] After a detailed study of the available data and the construction of several mathematical models intended to predict the future of college enrollments, the director of the Office of Program Planning and Evaluation, Office of Education comments: "The *removal of all financial constraints* has only a moderate effect on the number of students likely to attend institutions of higher education. . . . The effect is somewhat [more] pronounced for students who are likely to attend full time [rather than part time]." [3] The staff of the Commission on Human Resources and Advanced Education estimated that the removal of financial barriers "could presumably raise the proportion of poor but bright youth who complete college from 37 per cent to between 42 and 46 per cent." The increases for the not-so-bright would presumably be considerably less. The commission goes on to note:

To assume that simply by increasing financial support and opening up new educational opportunities we will automatically enable all bright but poor youth to attend college is naive. . . . Although loan and scholarship programs to assist in financing the post high school education of disadvantaged youth are necessary, they are not sufficient. If we are to solve the problem of filling society's needs for talented persons in high-level positions, we must intervene much earlier in the developmental history of the individual.[4]

I do not cite these sources in order to argue that students should not receive financial aid or that the increases in enrollment that would result are of no social value. I do it, rather, to suggest that reducing the financial barriers is not likely to have a dramatic effect on improving equality of access to the higher-

2 G. Nash, "Student Financial Aid—College and University."

3 J. Froomkin, *Aspirations, Enrollments, and Resources: The Challenge to Higher Education in the Seventies.* [Emphasis added.]

4 J. K. Folger, H. S. Astin, and A. E. Bayer, *Human Resources and Higher Education*, pp. 322–323. The primary focus of the commission was on the development of intellectual talent rather than on equality of opportunity.

education system, much less on the overall societal structures of inequality of opportunity.

For those who are skeptical of arguments documented only with quotes from "authorities," let us briefly review some of the reasons that financial aid will probably have less effect than most political and policy discussions would imply. First, a number of studies have found that when high school graduates are asked why they do not attend college, they infrequently give finances as the major reason. Of the 1970 high school graduates in New York City who did not attend college, only 10 per cent said they could not afford it. The researchers conclude, "The basic reason for nonapplication appears to be a lack of desire to continue education rather than the existence of barriers which prevented motivated students from considering college attendance." [5] A Census Bureau study based on a national sample of the high school graduates of 1966 came to a similar conclusion. Of those who came from families making more than five thousand dollars, 10 per cent mentioned finances as the main reason for not attending college while the figure was 18 per cent for those whose families made less than five thousand dollars.[6] In sum, the first reason that financial aid is not likely to increase equality of opportunity significantly is that lack of money is not the primary barrier to lower-class high school graduates. Such factors as academic preparation and motivation seem to be much more important.

The second reason is that much (if not most) of this aid does not go to those who have the greatest financial need. It has long been recognized that the low-tuition state schools stimulate enrollments from the middle class more than from the lower class. The percentage of 1969 freshmen enrolled in four-year colleges who came from families making less than four thousand dollars was 6.0 per cent for public institutions, 5.4 per cent for nonsectarian private colleges, 7.1 per cent for Protestant colleges, and 3.8 per cent for Catholic institutions. In other words, low-tuition publicly supported colleges—the most com-

    [5] R. Birnbaum and J. Goldman, *The Graduates: A Follow-Up Study of New York City High School Graduates of 1970*, p. 6.
    [6] Froomkin, p. 21.

mon form of "financial aid"—do not enroll significantly larger numbers of students from the low socioeconomic groups than other types of institutions. Private universities actually enrolled slightly more low-income freshmen than public universities— 3.7 per cent compared with 3.4 per cent from families making less than four thousand dollars.[7]

To a lesser degree, this pattern (most of the assistance going to the middle class) also holds for two-year colleges. Research done in the Office of Program Planning and Evaluation of the Office of Education finds that: "Junior colleges tend to attract lower income students as compared to four-year institutions. Yet, if enrollment patterns of the mid-1960's are to be credited, they do not enroll proportionately very many more students from the lowest income quartile." [8] This picture held through the end of the 1960s. In 1969, public two-year colleges enrolled 7.5 per cent of their students from families making less than four thousand dollars, while as we have seen earlier, the figure for public four-year colleges was 6.0 per cent.

Some have even argued that state-supported public colleges and universities are actually a regressive form of tax-supported service. That is, the poor get a lower proportion of the subsidies, relative to the taxes they pay, than the rich. Even if this contention is an overstatement, tax-supported institutions at best provide only a very modest redistribution of resources.[9]

What about other forms of financial aid? Most forms of tax relief provide little, if any, benefit to lower income groups. For example, a tax relief program advocated by Senator Abraham Ribicoff is estimated to provide $524 million in assistance to the top income quartile, $301 million to the second quartile, $122 million to the third quartile, and nothing to the lowest income quartile.

[7] American Council on Education, *National Norms for College Freshman—Fall 1969*, p. 39.
[8] Froomkin, p. 25.
[9] See for example W. L. Hansen and B. A. Weisbrod, *Benefits, Costs, and Finance of Public Higher Education*, and J. A. Pechman, "The Distributional Effects of Public Higher Education in California," *Journal of Human Resources*, 1970, 5, 361–370.

A large percentage of traditional forms of financial aid—grants, loans, and work-study programs—are administered by the financial-aid offices of the individual colleges and universities. This is true even for most state and federally supported student aid programs. Compared to subsidized tuition and tax relief a higher proportion of these forms of aid tends to be distributed to those who have the greatest need. For example, in 1966–1967, the student loan program under the National Defense Education Act provided forty million dollars to the top income quartile and sixty-nine million dollars to the lowest quartile. The federal work-study program provided six million dollars to the top quartile and a hundred and two million dollars to the bottom income quartile. The educational opportunity grants (scholarships) gave out one million dollars in benefits to students in the highest quartile, and thirty-three million dollars to the lowest income group.[10]

Granting that the scholarship, loan, and work-study programs administered by the colleges and universities distribute financial aid in a relatively progressive fashion, definite tendencies nonetheless exist for aid not to be distributed strictly according to need. Traditionally, aid has been used by institutions as a means of attracting talented students. High school graduates with outstanding academic records were offered scholarships in an attempt to attract them to that institution. This practice was especially prevalent among the high-status colleges and universities. In the early 1950s educational institutions realized that this type of competition for students was largely self-defeating and was a poor use of limited aid funds. Consequently, in 1954, the College Entrance Examination Board, which had been founded to develop standardized entrance examinations, established the College Scholarship Service. Since that time, this organization has developed a standard form and procedure for calculating a student's financial need and the amount of aid he should receive. For nearly twenty years, the College Scholarship Service has attempted to rationalize its system and to see that assistance was granted primarily according to need.

[10] US Office of Education, *Students and Buildings*, p. 18.

Some progress has undoubtedly been made in this direction. Yet despite these years of effort, there is still a definite tendency to distribute aid according to other criterion than need. The College Scholarship Service itself commissioned a Panel of Student Financial Need Analysis, chaired by Allan M. Cartter, chancellor of New York University and one of the recognized authorities on highly trained manpower. The panel found that in about half of the institutions that were studied, "large financial need significantly reduced the probability of acceptance, *even when quantifiable indicators of ability were used as controls.*" [11] It also found that the higher the total financial need of the student (as estimated by the institutions according to a rather sophisticated standard formula), the lower the percentage that was actually met by student aid. For example, the middle-class student who has an estimated financial need of several hundred dollars may have most or all of this need met by the student aid he is granted. In contrast the lower class student who may need several thousand dollars in order to pay for college will frequently receive aid covering a much smaller portion of this total estimated need. Finally, the panel found that those from the lower class with high financial needs were only slightly more likely to receive larger grants (as contrasted with loans and jobs) than those with lesser needs. Grants tended to be awarded according to ability rather than need. The panel concludes that "the students most likely to be excluded from higher education by insufficient financial aid are those with the highest need. Students from low-income families are also the students who without question seem to fare the worst through the system currently operating. At each step of the process, the high-need student does not receive aid up to the need level established by the College Scholarship Service norms." [12]

The above discussion of financial aid is not intended as even an adequate summary of the overall state of financial assistance to college students, much less as a comprehensive discussion of the issue. Most of the qualifying details are left out

[11] College Entrance Examination Board, *Report of the Panel on Student Financial Need Analysis.*
[12] CEEB.

and the discussion deliberately focuses on the weakness of financial aid as a means of reducing inequality and inequality of opportunity. But even if the above discussion is deliberately biased, it is hopefully not a distortion. The purpose of the discussion has been to bring into serious question what the Cartter panel has called the "cherished myth of educators and the general public . . . that student financial aid today is primarily based upon relative need." Only when this myth has been rejected will we be able to see fully both the possibilities and the limitations of student financial aid.

A brief postscript is in order concerning why financial aid is not distributed according to need. The reader should not assume that this situation is due primarily to the venality, stupidity, or middle-class prejudices of deans and college financial-aid officers, although the last two may play some role. The major reasons for this situation are a series of institutional dilemmas and constraints. For example, students who want and deserve aid always exceed available funds. Consequently, a financial-aid officer can help several middle-class students with modest but genuine needs for the same amount of money that he can help one lower-class student who will need a large amount of aid. Moreover, the aid officer knows that the lower-class student is less likely to complete his college education even if all of his aid needs are met. Although expanding the amount of available aid may help, it will not eliminate this problem. Second, all organizations tend to be concerned about the quality of their output and their status relative to similar organizations. A key determinant of the quality of a college or university's graduates and of its own organizational status is the quality of the students admitted (a fact college administrators seem to have known intuitively for a long time). Consequently, admissions and financial-aid officers are under almost unavoidable institutional pressure to recruit high-ability students through the use of student aid. Such a tendency need be neither an explicit policy nor even a conscious procedure. It is probably enough for the admissions and aid officers to have a strong concern about the long-term welfare of their institution for there to be a bias—in outcome if not in intent—in favor of high-ability students and against lower-class students.[13] This source of bias is probably not going to be eliminated without a radical reorganization of the student-aid process, if not the educational system (or even society!) as a whole.

I have suggested that an expansion of student aid is likely to have less effect on equality of opportunity than is frequently supposed, first because lack of money is not the primary barrier to college attendance by underprivileged high school graduates and second because a surprising portion of student aid tends to go to the middle class rather than the lower class. A third reason is a possible tendency for the higher-education system to become more internally stratified as it includes greater numbers of individuals. Considerable variation has always existed in the academic prestige of the various colleges and universities and the degrees they granted. However, status differences have been informal, continuous, and ambiguous rather than discrete and explicit. Consequently, graduates of lower quality schools were not treated in a completely different manner than others. During the 1960s there was a tendency to formalize some of these status differences. Some publicly supported systems, California for example, have drawn a formal distinction between universities, senior colleges, and junior colleges. Each of these levels is seen as carrying out at least somewhat different functions and consequently varying with respect to curriculum and level of performance expected. One can readily imagine how the job market might come to draw clear-cut distinctions between the graduates of these different types of colleges in the same way that colleges have in the past drawn clear, if informal, distinctions between the graduates of academic high schools and the graduates of vocational or general high schools.

Such a differentiation process could in large measure cancel out the effects of additional financial aid because, as we have seen, there is a very strong tendency for students from low socioeconomic backgrounds to enroll in lower prestige institutions. As the Commission on Human Resources report notes:

[13] For a discussion of the effects of selectivity on institutional quality, see A. Astin, "Undergraduate Achievement and Institutional Excellence," *Science*, Aug. 16, 1968; and Froomkin, Chap. 5.

"If the selectivity gap between our major universities and our open-door two-year colleges widens further, . . . students who initially enter the open-door colleges may find it difficult to make the transition to the major universities which largely control access to the prestige professions." [14] I am not arguing that the internal differentiation and stratification of the higher-education system is inevitable. However, it seems at least as reasonable to expect this outcome as to assume that further expansion of the higher-education system will bring a significant and genuine increase in equality of opportunity.

In conclusion, I doubt that increased aid will significantly change the structure of inequality or opportunity. This is not to argue that new forms of financial aid and new procedures of administration are impossible or, much less, useless. But if research and previous experience are useful guidelines to the future—and admittedly they sometimes are not—there is room for skepticism and pessimism. In closing this part of the discussion, let me quote the observations of William Sewell, former president of the American Sociological Association, who has done extensive research on the factors affecting college attendance and completion.

The present generation of students at the better universities is composed largely of urban, middle- and upper-class youth. Although the trend has been for an increasing proportion of children from rural and urban blue-collar backgrounds to attend college, my own studies indicate that only a small minority of farm and working-class youth pursue higher education in the better universities. Those who do attend are for the most part enrolled in vocationally oriented courses—engineering, business, and agriculture. Our failure to provide the motivation and means for the admission of able lower-class youth into the top levels of our system of higher education is not only a pressing problem for higher education, it is an indictment against society's commitment to equality of opportunity. [15]

[14] Folger, Astin, and Bayer, p. 196.
[15] W. H. Sewell, "Students and the University," *The American Sociologist*, 1971, *6*, 111–112.

My thesis has been that although some forms of financial aid will affect social mobility to a limited degree, no form of aid will change the patterns of mobility sufficiently to have significant effects either on equality of opportunity or on equality in the societal stratification system. Up to this point, two lines of argument have been suggested to support this thesis.

First, we have seen that SES affects not only the transition from high school to initial college enrollment, but continues to influence an individual's life chances throughout the higher-education process. Even if student aid significantly increased the enrollment rates of low-SES students, it would not nearly equalize the chances in terms of total educational, occupational, and income attainment.

The second line of argument focused on whether increased levels of financial aid to students would increase low-SES enrollments and educational attainment. Most studies suggest that they would have a very modest impact. The most we can say at this point is that aid would help somewhat, but probably not very much.

Past Trends

Now I want to present a third line of argument. In this section we are going to look at the historical trends in educational attainment and opportunity and compare these with historical trends in social mobility and equality in the societal stratification structure. In essence, the findings are that although educational attainment has increased greatly for all social classes, the distribution of years of schooling has equalized somewhat, and the occupational structure has undergone dramatic changes, social mobility and the income distribution have remained almost unchanged. I would be hesitant to base any conclusions on the comparisons of such gross trends if previous chapters had not examined some of the intervening social processes and brought into serious question whether they will be efficacious in bringing about changes in the *relative* educational attainment of various socioeconomic classes. The argument here is that using federal aid to expand college enrollments—even of low-SES students—is another round in the long history of expanding education and using the prospect of increased opportunity and equality as part of the justification for this expansion. Although such expansion has undoubtedly had other effects on American society, the evidence does not show that it has significantly increased equality or equality of opportunity.

First, let us examine trends in educational attainment. That steady increases in the level of educational attainment have occurred is well known. The average (median) number of years of schooling (for those 25 and over) was 8.1 in 1910 and increased steadily until in 1970 Americans averaged 12.2 years of schooling. In other words, in the last sixty years, the average level of education shifted from completion of elementary school to the completion of high school. Averages for the total population do not, of course, reflect the present norms or expectations because most of the people included in the averages finished their formal schooling many years before. Consequently, we also find it useful to look at changes in the school retention rates. These retention rates tell us how many individuals of a given age group have progressed to any specified level in the educational system. For example, for each hundred students who entered the fifth grade in 1930, retention rates will indicate how many entered the eighth grade in 1933, graduated from high school in 1938, and so on. These retention rates also show a picture of steady increases in the years of schooling Americans received. For every hundred students who entered the fifth grade in 1925, seventy-four completed the eighth grade, thirty graduated from high school, and twelve entered college. For the hundred students attending the fifth grade in 1960, ninety-eight completed the eighth grade, seventy-two completed high school, and forty entered college.[16] In other words, over a thirty-five-year period, the percentage of individuals graduating from high school more than doubled and the percentage going on to college more than tripled. As we shall see later in Part III, the rates of upward educational mobility also increased during this time period.

[16] US Office of Education, *Digest of Educational Statistics, 1969*, p. 7.

But if there was a significant expansion of the educational system and if the levels of educational attainment increased dramatically, there was no change in the influence of socioeconomic background on educational and occupational achievement. The average level of education increased, but equality of opportunity was not affected.

In 1962, the Bureau of the Census collected information on intergenerational mobility from a large national sample of men.[17] By breaking this large sample into age categories it was possible to analyze the influence of the father's social status on their son's social status for four different ten-year age cohorts. The youngest cohort graduated from high school during the period from approximately 1943 to 1952 while the oldest cohort would have completed high school between about 1913 and 1922. These data make it possible to correlate for each age group the relationship between three sets of factors: (1) father's education and son's education, (2) father's occupation and son's education, and (3) father's occupation and son's occupation.

An analysis of these data shows that the effect of the father's social status (education and occupation) on the son's social status is virtually the same for all four age groups. The strength of the correlations varies slightly for different age groups, but clearly the overall finding is no change. That is, there is no indication that an increase in the rigidity of the opportunity structure has occurred; but neither has there been an increase in equality of opportunity.

One of the minor variations over time suggests that financial aid is ineffective in producing equality of opportunity. Blau and Duncan comment:

It may be sheer coincidence that both [the correlation between father's occupation and son's education and the correlation between father's education and son's education] show the highest value for the 1933–1944 cohort. This cohort happens to be the one with by far the largest proportion (roughly three quarters)

[17] The most extensive analysis of these data is presented in P. M. Blau and O. D. Duncan, *The American Occupational Structure.*

*of its members veterans of World War II. Sociologists have
sometimes speculated that the availability of educational benefits
in the "G.I. Bill" may have equalized opportunities for men com-
ing from different socioeconomic backgrounds. The present data
contain no hint of such an equalization effect, which would have
reduced [the correlation], not enhanced it.*[18]

In sum, we find that the vast expansion in educational
facilities and attainment in the first half of the twentieth century
apparently had no measurable effect on equality of opportunity.
We grant, of course, that equality of opportunity would have
decreased if educational opportunities had not expanded. We will
return to this issue in Part III.

A final note about the trends in inequality (as distinct
from opportunity). The data on trends in the distribution of
wealth and income are complex and ambiguous. We need only
note here that the prevailing view is that the distribution of income has remained roughly constant since World War II.

We have some indication that the distribution of the years
of schooling has become more equal. That is, the distance between the least educated and the best educated has decreased.
Calculations by Jencks and Riesman show that between 1875 and
1885, the third of the population with the most education had
acquired about 53 per cent of the total years of schooling for the
whole society. By 1930–1934 this figure had dropped to 43 per
cent. Comparing these same years, the percentage of the total
years of schooling going to the least educated third of the population shifted from thirteen to twenty-two. As Jencks and Riesman point out, the later years of schooling cost many times more
per student than the earlier years. Consequently, the distribution
of educational resources—in contrast to years of schooling—has
been equalized considerably less. Although there are no reliable
data, they guess that the distribution of educational resources has
remained approximately stable.[19] Consequently, the expansion of
education has had no obvious effect on income inequality per se,

18 Blau and Duncan, p. 179.
19 Jencks and Reisman, p. 82.

and probably only a small effect on the distribution of educational resources per se. We will consider changes in the degree of inequality in a little more detail in Part III.

Conclusion

The past expansion of education has had no apparent effect on mobility, and consequently the degree of inequality and inequality of opportunity have remained roughly constant. The two previous conclusions were that socioeconomic background continues to affect achievement significantly after college enrollment and that expanded student aid has at best a moderate effect on lower-class college enrollment. When we link these three conclusions together, it seems much more reasonable to predict that the expansion of student-aid programs will have little effect on social opportunity and equality than to assume the opposite. For some time, we have been pushing on the rock that is the stratification system with the long limber rod of educational opportunity. Considering the lack of movement in the past, it seems doubtful that pushing a little harder will make much difference in the future.

Racial Inequality

Six

In the past two chapters, we have argued that financial aid to students will do relatively little to equalize the opportunities available to those from differing socioeconomic backgrounds. Now we turn to the question of whether student aid will help reduce racial inequality—and a seeming paradox presents itself. In regard to this question, I will argue the opposite of what I argued in Chapters 4 and 5 concerning class inequality. That is, I will argue that financial aid can, in the long run, significantly help to raise the educational, occupational, and income levels and improve the life chances of black [1] Americans. First, the data

---

[1] "Black" and "Negro" are used interchangeably. When "nonwhite" is used its meaning is identical to the definition used by the U.S. Census: The nonwhite group includes Negroes, Indians, Japanese, Chinese and other nonwhite races. Negroes composed about 90 percent of the nonwhite category, and the latter category is frequently used as a surrogate for the former one.

to support the line of argument will be presented. Then, a theoretical basis for resolving the apparent contradiction will be outlined.

In the preceding chapters, we saw that even if student financial aid is effective in increasing college attendance rates for lower-class high school graduates, the gain is overshadowed by a series of countervailing social processes within the larger educational and occupational structure. Consequently, in our consideration of racial equality, we will examine these larger social processes first. After we have seen the context and limits they set on the movement toward racial equality, we will take up the question of the effects of student aid for black college students.

The essence of the argument hinges on the observation that the expansion of subsidized education—whether it be through low-tuition state schools or aid to individual students—has allowed Negroes to increase their levels of education at a rate considerably faster than that of whites. In contrast, lower-class whites have been able to increase their absolute level of education but not at a rate fast enough to close the gap significantly and overtake members of the upper class. The second key point of the argument is that racial discrimination in the job market seems to be decreasing fairly rapidly—at least for black college graduates—thereby enabling Negroes with higher education to obtain jobs with a status and income similar to whites with the same level of education. To put it another way, blacks are increasingly able to translate educational gains into gains in occupational status and income.

Closing the Gap

That blacks are underprivileged relative to whites is obvious. In 1970, for example, nonwhite median family income was $6,516 compared with $10,236 for whites.[2] Our interest is not, however, in the current degree of racial inequality but in the past trends and future prospects.

Negroes, like whites, have had substantial and steady in-

[2] US Bureau of the Census, "Income in 1970 of Families and Persons in the United States," *Current Population Reports,* P-60 (80).

creases in the absolute level of their incomes, at least since the end of the Depression. However, between the end of World War II and the middle of the 1960s there was virtually no change in the relative gap between the incomes of blacks and whites. The average nonwhite income was slightly over 50 per cent of the average white income throughout this period.[3] In short, the degree of inequality remained virtually the same.

Essentially, the same situation held for occupational differences. Negroes participated in the general upgrading of the occupational structure. Like whites, they increased their numbers in the professional, clerical, and service occupations and moved out of farming and laborers' jobs. Unlike whites the percentage of black craftsmen and operatives (primarily factory workers) increased and the percentage that were household servants decreased. Although some managed to move into white-collar jobs, apparently movement into the higher blue-collar jobs vacated by upwardly mobile whites was also common. But as with income, the relative distance between blacks and whites remained much the same during the twenty years following World War II. For example, the index of occupational dissimilarity was forty-one in 1950, forty in 1955, forty-three in 1960, and thirty-eight in 1966.[4] In some years during this period, the gap was reduced, but there was no definite long-term trend toward greater equality.[5]

In contrast to the gap in income and jobs, the gap between white and Negro levels of education was reduced considerably between 1950 and 1965. For example, in 1950, the average num-

        [3] US Bureau of the Census, "Income in 1967 of Families in the United States," *Current Population Reports*, P-60 (59).
        [4] This index indicates the percentage of nonwhites that would have to change occupational categories, that is, move up in the occupational structure, in order to have the same occupational distribution as whites. For example, in 1950, 41 per cent of the nonwhites would have had to move into a higher status occupational category for blacks to be represented in each occupation in proportion to their representation in the total work force.
        [5] US Bureau of the Census, *Statistical Abstract of the United States*, 1968, p. 226; and *Statistical Abstract of the United States, 1969*, p. 223.

ber of years of schooling for those 25–29—generally considered
to be the youngest age group to have "finished school"—was
12.2 for whites and 8.7 for nonwhites. In 1965, the figures were
12.5 years for whites and 12.0 years for nonwhites. In other
words, by the last half of the 1960s, young adult blacks were
on the average staying in school 96 per cent as long as their
white peers.[6] Moreover, there has been a long history of steady
reductions in the gap between black and white levels of education. For example, in 1890, nonwhites (25–29 years old) were
on the average receiving only 19 per cent as many years of
schooling as whites. This percentage has steadily increased until
in 1970 the figure was about 97 per cent. (Data covering the
entire period from 1890 to 1970 is presented in Table 2 in Chapter 8.)

Two qualifications are in order about the changes since
World War II. When we looked at trends in income and occupational differences, we used figures for the total adult population, while the figures for education were for the 25–29 age
group. If we compared the income and occupational differences
of young whites and young blacks as we did for education, we
might find greater gains in equality than the figures for the total
population indicate. However, even with this refinement, the
reductions in job and income differences would not have nar-
rowed nearly as dramatically as the differences in schooling.
Second, the quality of the schools attended by blacks is on the
average lower than the quality of schools attended by whites.
But this discrepancy existed both at the beginning and at the end
of the period so that the changes observed are real ones, even if
the figures for any one year understate the degree of inequality.

Although the average levels of education for blacks and
whites became more similar, such a convergence did not occur
at the college level between the mid-1950s and the mid-1960s.
In other words, the averages were affected primarily by increases
in the percentage of blacks that were completing elementary
and high school. The higher-education gap remained about the

[6] US Office of Education, *Digest of Educational Statistics, 1970*,
p. 9.

same or even increased. For example, in 1964, the ratio of black to white college graduates for the 25-29 age group (most of whom were in college between 1957 and 1961) was .41. That is, blacks graduated from college at a rate that was only 41 per cent of the white rate of graduation. The ratio for 1969 was .40, while the average for the four years between 1964 and 1969 (namely, 1965–1968) was .39. The dropout rates, for both the transition between high school and college and during college, tended to increase for blacks, especially males, while dropout rates tended to decrease for whites. It should be kept in mind that the 1964–1969 figures for the 25–29 age group primarily reflect what was happening five to ten years earlier.[7] More recently, this trend seems to have reversed itself, and blacks seem to be gaining on whites at the higher levels of education also. For example, in 1964, the college enrollment rate for blacks 18-24 years old was 37 per cent of the white rate. By 1968, the figure had increased to 53 per cent.[8] This increase means that blacks were still far behind whites at the college level but that they were catching up quickly.

The point of these somewhat tedious statistics on income, occupation, and education is to demonstrate that the gap in the educational levels of blacks and whites has been steadily closing, even when little progress was being made in other areas. Of special interest is that the gains in education were at the levels that are publicly financed. In contrast, little progress was made at the level of higher education where the cost to the student and his family is normally considerably more. Moreover—and this may be pure coincidence—blacks began to catch up at the college level about the time that the federal government began to increase expenditures on student financial aid. For example, in 1960, the National Defense Student Loan Program received about forty million dollars while by 1968, it received one hundred and eighty-two million dollars. In 1965, the federal work-study program was initiated with a twenty-one million dollar expenditure which

[7] These statistics are derived from US Bureau of the Census, *Current Population Reports*, P-20 (138, 158, 169, 182, and 194).

[8] US Bureau of the Census, "School Enrollment: October 1968 and 1967," *Current Population Reports*, P-20 (190), 4.

was increased to one hundred and twelve million by 1968. In 1967, the Equal Opportunity Grants (scholarships) Program was initiated with fifty million dollars and doubled the next year.[9] It would be a mistake to make too much out of the parallel between this expansion of financial aid to college students and the reduction in the gap between white and black college enrollment; yet the parallel certainly suggests that student aid contributes to reducing racial inequality. Later, we will consider why student aid may have a significant impact on black enrollments. Assuming for the moment that further progress is possible in closing the education gap, we must consider whether blacks will be able to translate their equal levels of education into equal jobs and incomes.

Does It Pay to Stay?

A great deal of emphasis has been placed in recent years on the importance of raising the educational level of minority-group members. Television commercials and bus and subway posters frequently emphasize the importance of staying in school and getting a good education. Conventional wisdom advises the minority group member who wants to advance himself to "learn, baby, learn." Yet some activists and researchers question whether staying in school pays off for blacks as much as is usually assumed. We have already seen that from the end of World War II until the mid-1960s, the gap between black and white occupational and income levels stayed about the same—despite significant reductions in educational differences.

In discussing this issue, we must distinguish between two questions. First: Do higher levels of education enable Negroes to secure better jobs? The answer to this question is obviously yes. For example, in March, 1970, 65 per cent of nonwhite men with four or more years of college were professionals or technical workers, while only 4 per cent of the high school graduates in the nonwhite male category had such jobs. The pattern was similar for other levels of education. Thirty-two per cent of

---

[9] US Office of Education, *Digest of Educational Statistics,* 1969, pp. 104–105.

nonwhite men with one to three years of college had clerical or sales jobs while the figure was 17 per cent for high school graduates and 7 per cent for high school dropouts.[10]

The second, and more important, question focuses on the differences between the occupational attainment of whites and nonwhites with the same levels of education. The problem is to determine the extent to which occupational differences between whites and blacks are the result of differences in education (and other universalistic criteria) or outright racial discrimination in hiring and promotion practices.

Occupational differences between blacks and whites with the same level of education generally decreased slightly between 1950 and 1960. However, the most basic and persistent pattern for the period was blacks having significantly lower status occupations than whites with the same level of education. Actually, the more education blacks had, the greater was the degree of job discrimination—unless they managed to finish college, in which case discrimination decreased by about 50 per cent. Moreover, for college graduates in the younger age groups, the occupational differences between blacks and whites increased slightly.[11]

Otis Dudley Duncan attempted to estimate the relative influence of three factors on occupational differences between white and nonwhite men using data collected in 1962.[12] Scoring occupations according to his socioeconomic index for all occupations, he found that the average occupational-status score for whites was nearly twice as high as the score for nonwhites. About 28 per cent of the gap was accounted for by differences in family background, namely, the tendency of nonwhites to have fathers with a lower level of educational and occupational status than whites. About 2 per cent of the difference was due to the tendency of nonwhites to have more siblings. Another 20 per cent of the occupational differences was accounted for by the tendency of nonwhites to have lower levels of education. Fifty per

[10] US Department of Labor, "Educational Attainment of Workers, March, 1969, 1970."

[11] P. M. Siegel, "On the Cost of Being a Negro," *Sociological Inquiry*, 1965, *35*, 41–57.

[12] O. D. Duncan, "Inheritance of Poverty or Inheritance of Race?"

cent of the difference remained unexplained. Although some of this unexplained residual difference may be due to factors such as geographical region, the quality of schooling received, and age, much is due to outright racial discrimination in hiring and promotion.

These findings could lead to the conclusion that attempts to reduce racial inequality through expansion of educational opportunities for blacks is a relatively poor investment which is likely to yield only small improvements. (Only 20 per cent of the differences in occupational level were due to differences in education.) In large measure, such a conclusion may be warranted. Despite the prevalent "learn, baby, learn" ideology, the basic reason blacks have poor jobs and low income is still white racism and not black incompetence.

However, evidence indicates that things may be changing. My own analysis of the data available between 1960 and 1970 indicates that since 1967, modest decreases in the occupational difference between whites and nonwhites seem to have occurred.[13] For example, the index of occupational dissimilarity was about 38 in 1966 and about 28 in 1970. Of even more interest, since 1962 the percentage of the black-white occupational differences that was due to lower levels of black education seems to have increased. In 1962, about 30 per cent of the occupational difference was caused by lower levels of black education whereas in 1970, the figure was 40 per cent. Such a trend may seem impossible because we have seen that during this same period the gap between black and white education was reduced considerably. This seeming paradox probably means that discrimination against blacks in the job market decreased at a faster rate than their levels of education increased. Consequently, all of the following assertions are true: (1) the occupation gap decreased, (2) the education gap decreased, but (3) a higher proportion of the remaining occupation gap is due to the remaining differences in education. Another change during the 1960-1970 period that is

[13] M. Milner, Jr., "Race, Education, and Jobs: Trends 1960–1970." Based on analysis of data presented in Table J of US Department of Labor, *Special Labor Force Reports*, Nos. 30, 65, 83, 92, 103, and 125.

significant to our concerns is that discrimination in the job market has decreased most for those with college training. This decrease in discrimination was especially true for those who had completed one to three years of training but had not obtained a degree. Blacks who go on to college will not only have better jobs than those with only high school training, but they will have jobs similar to those held by whites with college training.

Once again, qualifications are in order. The data and mode of analysis on which these findings are based are not precise and are therefore subject to measurement error and sampling error. More important, short-term trends of the type we are considering (four to eight years) have been misleading in the past. For example, Negroes made substantial gains during World War II but the trend did not continue after the war. The economic recession of 1970-1971 retarded, if not eliminated, the kinds of gains made during the 1960s. A long period of economic decline could prevent future progress and wipe out past gains.

Nonetheless, all things considered, the most reasonable prospect for the future is that blacks will increasingly be able to translate higher levels of education into equal jobs and equal income.

Will Financial Aid Help Blacks?

The last two sections have focused on the larger social processes. The findings suggest that the black-white educational gap can be further reduced and that Negro gains in education can be translated into gains in occupational status and income. Now we must examine the short-term question of whether expanded financial aid to black students will help to reduce further the education gap.

Let us begin on a negative note. Money is probably not the major bottleneck to increasing black educational attainment. Motivational and academic factors are more significant, as was the case for whites. Granting this, I still want to suggest that increased levels of financial aid will contribute significantly to reducing black-white educational differences and in turn other types of racial inequality and inequality of opportunity. Two lines of argument are relevant here. The first hinges on the difference between objective and subjective aspects of social class.

Taking the society as a whole, a very high percentage of blacks are, objectively speaking, in the lower class, for example in the lowest income quartile. This percentage also holds for college students. In 1968, 31 per cent of the black freshmen compared with 5 per cent of the nonblack freshmen came from families making less than four thousand dollars.[14] Consequently, insofar as membership in the lower class means that people do not have the money to pay for college—an objective handicap—a high percentage of blacks suffer this handicap. However, evidence indicates that the subjective aspects of social class which affect educational attainment are related not to the status position in the total society but to the position one holds within his own ethnic community. In other words, although most blacks are objectively poor and belong to the lower class, a significant percentage of them are, subjectively speaking, of the middle class—at least with respect to the factors which influence college enrollment. For example, when Abram J. Jaffe and Walter Adams reanalyzed the data from the Coleman report, they found "that minority students of both sexes are considerably more likely than majority ones to wish to excell" in their academic work. When ability was held constant, this difference increased because desire to excel is related to high measured ability and there are proportionately fewer high-ability minority students than white students. They concluded that blacks (and whites) formed their self-image, academic desire, and plans in reference to their relative performance within their own ethnic community.[15]

Consequently, eliminating objective handicaps such as racial discrimination and inadequate financial resources is likely to have more impact on this population than on the population of whites with comparable levels of income. A high proportion of the blacks are, subjectively speaking, middle class; what they have lacked is opportunity and money.

Of course, this line of argument must be immediately

[14] American Council on Education, *The Black Student in American Colleges*, ACE Research Report, 1969, 4 (2).

[15] A. J. Jaffe and W. Adams, *American Higher Education in Transition*, p. 61.

qualified. Obviously, Negroes who are middle class in terms of the internal structure of the black community are not psychologically the same as members of the white middle class. Even relatively well-off blacks have suffered tremendous deprivations that have affected both their motivation for achievement and their skills. Apparently, even middle-class blacks have traditionally had very negative self-images which undercut their motivation and performance. But the cultural changes symbolized by the phrase "black is beautiful" may have done much to eliminate this handicap for members of the black community who are relatively well off. In the future, the positive influence of being middle class within the black community may have a greater effect on a Negro's self-image than any negative feelings about being black. In fact, it is possible that many "middle-class" blacks may, because of racial pride, have a more positive self-image than middle-class whites—even though the latter is likely to rank higher by objective measures such as income.

The second line of argument is based upon the observation that within the black community education has traditionally been the most important criterion of prestige and status. That is, an individual's education was a more important factor in determining his overall prestige than other factors such as income, occupation, and moral behavior.[16]

Other factors such as occupation and income are also, of course, very important—and are probably becoming relatively more important—but traditionally, education seems to have been given more weight than these other factors. This has not been true in the white community where occupation and income have been more important than education in determining an individual's prestige. Apparently the primary reason for this difference is that within the black community there has been greater variation in educational level than in income and occupational status. The range of variation for occupations and incomes was relatively narrow: nearly all blacks had low income and occupational

[16] See N. G. Glenn, "Negro Prestige Criteria: A Case Study in the Bases of Prestige," *American Journal of Sociology*, 1963, *68*, 645–657. Glenn surveys sixteen empirical studies of prestige in Negro communities between 1899 and 1960.

status. There has been considerably more variation in education. Because of Negro colleges and a significant number of unsegregated institutions in the North, blacks have had easier access to the higher levels of education than they have had to high incomes or prestigious occupations. Those with ambition and talent could distinguish themselves by educational accomplishments. In contrast ambition and talent were of relatively little help in overcoming job and income discrimination. There was an implicit ceiling on the occupations and incomes that blacks were allowed to have, and very few managed to break through this barrier.

Since education is a more important source of social status for blacks than whites, it is reasonable to expect that this would increase their motivation to obtain education. Earlier I argued that a black child from a given objective level in the stratification system would tend to have a higher motivation for education than white children from the same objective level. This would be so because the black child would come from a family having a higher relative position within the Negro community—and therefore would subjectively speaking have a higher socioeconomic status than whites with the same objective position. (This is based on the assumption that there tends to be a significant association between high subjective status and motivation for education.) This second line of argument—that education is a more important basis of prestige for blacks—suggests that even at the same relative (subjective) position, blacks might have a higher motivation for education. For example, the black youth whose family's income was close to the median level for blacks might be more motivated to seek a college education than the white youth whose family's income was close to the median level for whites—even though the black child has the same subjective social status and a lower objective social status.

Admittedly, these two lines of argument are largely speculative, though they are supported by the findings of Jaffe and Adams mentioned above. They do suggest theoretical reasons why student financial aid might have a significantly greater effect on eliminating racial differences in educational attainment than on eliminating class differences.

The factor that makes the effectiveness of financial aid

most problematic is academic ability. It has been documented repeatedly that blacks score significantly lower (about one standard deviation) than whites on standardized measures of IQ and achievement. There is a heated debate over how much of this difference is due to genetic factors and how much is due to environmental differences.[17] Whatever the source of these measured differences, they will contribute to the difficulty in eliminating the gap in educational attainment. Nonetheless it seems to me that the most convincing evidence that this and other handicaps can be overcome, at least to some extent, is the steady progress that has already been made in reducing educational differences. Because of the factors outlined above, I think that expanded financial aid will make a significant contribution to this process. I must add, however, that this conclusion is tentative and problematic.

To summarize: my thesis has been that expansion of federal aid to higher education is likely to help reduce racial inequality, although probably not class inequality. This conclusion was based primarily on two findings. First, Negroes have been successful in increasing their level of educational attainment at significantly higher rates than whites. Consequently, the average educational gap between younger blacks and whites has been reduced considerably. In contrast, the gap between lower- and upper-class whites has been reduced comparatively little. That is, attempts to reduce racial inequality by raising the level of Negro education are not offset by comparable increases in white attainment, that is, cancelled out by what was labelled in the first chapters as status inflation. From this observation—based primarily on processes occurring at the high school level—it seems reasonable that similar results will occur at the college level as higher education becomes more accessible.

The second basis for my conclusion is that the primary

[17] The literature on this debate is extensive and growing daily. The following include some of the more important references: B. Eckland, "Genetics and Sociology: A Reconsideration," *American Sociological Review*, 1967, 32, 173–194; *Environment, Heredity, and Intelligence, Harvard Educational Review*, reprint Series, (2); S. Scarr-Salapatek, "Race, Social Class, and IQ," *Science*, 174, 1285–1295.

bottleneck to equality of occupational status—discriminatory hiring and promotion practices—seems to be lessening, especially for Negroes with college training. Whether the same thing holds for income is not clear, but employers will probably be unable to maintain pay discrimination (less money for the identical work) where job discrimination is significantly reduced since the former by itself is highly visible. At any rate, Negroes who are able to obtain a college education during the next decade will probably be able to move much closer to occupational and income equality with whites than has been possible in the past or than will be possible for Negroes with lower levels of education.

On the basis of these findings, I conclude that increases in the number of Negroes who attend and graduate from college will make a significant contribution to the general reduction of racial inequality. This conclusion is based on the assumption that job and pay discrimination will continue to decrease. Consequently, the argument is not that higher education is the single key to equality. Rather, if other types of efforts, such as fair-employment programs, are maintained,[18] increasing the number of Negro college graduates will, relative to other alternatives, produce a high payoff in a short time with a minimum of political resistance. This is in contrast to programs at lower levels of schooling which obviously will require longer to produce a payoff in the stratification structure per se.

In short, the conclusion is that the larger social processes will permit expansion of Negro higher education to have a significant impact on reducing racial inequality in the society as a whole. Finally, I have argued—in a more tentative way—that financial aid will have a greater impact on blacks than on lower-class whites. Consequently, the expansion of financial aid to blacks will significantly raise their enrollment and advancement in higher education. Now let us return to the seeming paradox that expanded opportunities for higher education will reduce racial inequality but not class inequality or inequality of opportunity.

[18] Obviously, increasing their impact would increase the impact of expanded higher education.

Class Equality Versus Racial Equality

In this chapter, we have discussed racial inequality in terms of differences in education, occupation, and income. We used these same indicators to measure (and in a sense define) socioeconomic status (SES) when we discussed class inequality. Therefore, to show that blacks rank low on these indicators is to show that a larger percentage of these individuals are from the lower socioeconomic strata. Because we argue that financial aid to college students has relatively little impact on social mobility or equality with respect to SES, it may seem intuitively contradictory to argue that aid can have a significant effect on improving the SES of Negroes—even though the data presented support the argument. But the contradiction is more apparent than real, for there is a basic difference in the social processes involved. Complete equality of opportunity for all social classes requires that every individual in each generation be provided the same life chances as every other individual of the same generation. Those who start on the bottom must have the same chances for attaining high status as those who were born into the upper class. For a society to even approximate these conditions, it must maintain extremely high rates of mobility. If the social distance between the top and the bottom is great, many individuals will have to move a long distance *each generation.* To put it another way, the mobility [19] of one generation is not cumulative to the

[19] More accurately, circulation or net mobility. Intergenerational mobility can be broken down into two components: structural mobility and circulation mobility. Structural mobility refers to the intergenerational changes that occur because of changes in the structure of the stratification system, namely, the occupational structure. If white-collar workers constitute a much higher percentage of the total work force in the sons' generation than they did in their fathers' time, many sons will necessarily be upwardly mobile. Such intergenerational changes are referred to as structural mobility. Circulation mobility refers to intergenerational changes above and beyond the structural changes. Structural changes are not related to the question of equality of opportunity. The focus of this latter concept is not on how many sons have higher status jobs than their fathers, but whether the sons from low origins have the same life chances as the sons from high origins. This latter question is dependent not on total mobility or structural mobility but on the rates and patterns of circulation mobility.

mobility of the next generation since by definition someone is always on the bottom (at least unless perfect equality is attained).

Attaining complete racial equality is less demanding with respect to the amount of social mobility required because the effects are cumulative from generation to generation. The process involves moving enough blacks up and enough whites down so that the two groups are equally distributed over the stratification structure. But this redistribution can be done by accumulating movements over relatively short social distances for several generations until the association between race and low SES is eliminated. I am not arguing that it will be easy to reduce racial inequality but only that reducing class differences and their effects on the opportunities of each succeeding generation is much more difficult. Consequently, expansion of higher education is much more likely to be effective in producing the former than the latter.

Educational Inflation

The purpose of this rather long and somewhat tedious examination of the probable effect of increased financial aid for higher education has been twofold. First, I have tried to question the common assumption that putting more people into college somehow automatically contributes to equality and equality of opportunity. My purpose is not to suggest that expanded opportunities for higher education are bad or undesirable but rather to question a myth which has too long kept us from looking more closely at the real costs, benefits, limitations, and possibilities of schooling. Second, I have tried to examine in some detail the precise factors and mechanisms involved in one type of status inflation. As indicated earlier, other intervening factors and mechanisms operate in other types of status inflation. It remains for future research to elucidate these.

Another study of status inflation in the educational sector was carried out in recent years—although it was not conceived in these terms. Lelia Sussman studied the application of the American approach to equality of opportunity in Puerto Rico. Her findings are worth quoting at length.

Puerto Rico's postwar plunge into mass secondary and higher education, in imitation of the US pattern, has had several revealing consequences. First, the rapid expansion with limited resources led to a severe decline in the quality of the public high schools and the state University of Puerto Rico. Second, and surprisingly, the rate of attendance at twelfth grade for urban youths from upper, middle, and working classes was very nearly equal by 1960, even though only a third of the age group was enrolled at the secondary level. The children of the upper social strata had nothing like the disproportionate number of places in secondary education that they had in Europe and the US at an equivalent stage of growth in secondary enrollments. Third, this democratization of access was accomplished by increasing segregation of the socially advantaged and disadvantaged into the private and public sectors respectively and by a growing divergence of academic achievement between the two sectors. There is evidence that segregation is extending into higher education.

Thus, despite equalization of access to high school, there is very unequal access to high schools of superior quality. Class differentials in educational achievement remain large and significant. The Puerto Rican case also shows that self-segregation into separate schools of the socially and educationally advantaged for the purpose of maintaining their advantage has no necessary connection with race. In the Commonwealth, it is a class phenomena, not a racial one.[20]

In short, Sussman also found that the progress toward equality of opportunity was modest at best and that the recalcitrant problem is class inequality and inequality of opportunity rather than racial inequality.

But why does equality of opportunity for various social classes seem to be a more elusive goal than racial equality? This paradox seems strange in light of the relatively noncontroversial nature of the former and the great heat and bitterness that has

[20] L. Sussman, "Democratization and Class Segregation in Puerto Rican Schooling: US Model Transplanted," *Sociology of Education*, 1968, *41*, 321–342.

been generated by the latter. The reason for both the progress and the conflict is the same; in the realm of racial inequality, we are clearly committed—however tardily, reluctantly, and hypo-critically—to move toward racial *equality*. However, we are *not* committed to a policy of reducing class inequality. In fact, such a goal is frequently considered "socialistic," "Communistic," un-American, or worse. Instead, we continue to seek after an am-biguously defined concept of equality of opportunity and attempt to implement this elusive goal by further expansion of our educational system. If such a policy has not been successful in producing the intended effect, it has not been without its con-sequences. Part III focuses on some of these unintended conse-quences.

Decline
and Reemergence
of Social Conflict

Seven

In Part I, the focus was on the general process of status inflation and on its causes and consequences. Part II attempted to analyze in considerable detail the expansion of higher education as an example of status inflation in one sector of American society.

Part III will relate the process of status inflation and the expansion of education to aspects of social conflict and social change. The problem is to explain alternating periods of social conflict and social stability. The analysis begins with the Marxian scenario in which capitalist societies, including the US, are to be subjected to increasing levels of class conflict and eventually a violent revolution by the proletariat. Then we will consider several revised scenarios. These revisions tend to stress factors which have prevented conflict and revolution and have produced relative political stability in twentieth-century capitalist societies, especially in the United States. Then we will consider recent social conflicts and instability which have characterized American society. Finally, I attempt to suggest a unified interpretation for the American experience, an interpretation which accounts for relative stability followed by a new instability.

In the process of sketching out this line of argument, I will need to summarize, in condensed form, aspects of the social theories of Karl Marx and Max Weber. These summaries are presented primarily for those readers who are not professional social scientists in order to assist them in making the connection between these social theories and more contemporary analyses. The summaries necessarily involve considerable abbreviation and simplification. In the one or two instances where fine points do seem critical to the argument, some additional details are presented.

Damnation: Marxian Forecast

Marx's predictions about the future course of capitalist societies center on two sets of ideas. The first is based on assumptions about the interplay between the expansion of capital (in general and technology in particular) and increased levels of competition in the market. Marx argued that in order to remain competitive in the market, the capitalist will steadily introduce more efficient methods of production and organize larger and larger production units. In the process, an increasing number of capitalists will be driven out of business and become wage laborers who work for the remaining capitalists. As a result, a smaller and smaller percentage of the population will be capitalists and a larger and larger percentage will be workers. The second set of ideas predicts that at the same time the workers will tend to become more and more alienated until eventually the alienated workers, who are the overwhelming majority of the population, will revolt against the small number of remaining capitalists.

On the whole, Marx seems to have been correct in his predictions about the first process. The bulk of economic production is now carried out by enormous corporations rather than family firms. The consolidation process may have been slightly less malevolent than Marx anticipated—involving mergers and one capitalist buying out another rather than firms simply going broke—but the result is the same. The corollary is that fewer and fewer people are classified as self-employed. Relatively few independent capitalist entrepreneurs who own their own means of production and compete in the market for profits still exist. Although many of those who fall outside this category might object to being labelled wage laborers or workers, their role in the economy comes close to what Marx meant by these terms.

The controversy about Marx's predictions centers on whether alienation has accompanied the process of consolidation and on the specific social mechanisms that produce this alienation. I will make no attempt to compile a complete list of the processes which Marx anticipated would produce alienation, but I will mention a few of his key ideas. First, Marx thought that the level of skill required by workers would decrease. He anticipated the work force becoming more and more homogeneous as men were transformed into adjuncts of the machines they operated. Second, he predicted that economic crises would result with increasing severity and that unemployment would undercut whatever economic security the workers had. Third, he believed that because of labor-saving technology and unemployment, the economic level of the workers would deteriorate and that they would experience "increasing misery." As we shall see momentarily, the exact nature of this increasing misery is complex and ambiguous. Fourth, Marx predicted that because of the greater insecurity and misery, the level of conflict between the capitalists and workers would become more frequent and bitter and would involve violence and repression. Finally, he envisioned that the process would culminate in a violent revolution.

Let us for a moment back up and deal with one of the fine points of Marx's analysis. I have said that Marx predicted that the workers would suffer increasing misery. Unfortunately, exactly what Marx meant by this phrase is unclear, or, more accurately, he seems to have meant different things at different times. In his early works, namely, the *Communist Manifesto*, he implies that the absolute economic position of the workers will deteriorate and that their standard of living will be lowered. In his later works, namely, *Capital* and *Wages, Price, and Profit*, he seems to mean that the workers' *relative* economic position will decline; their wages and standard of living may increase, but the distance between the workers and the capitalists will increase. In these later discussions, the emphasis seems to be on relative deprivation rather than absolute deprivation. Whichever interpretation we accept regarding Marx's theory of increasing misery, he predicted that either would contribute significantly to the alienation of the working class.[1]

Redemption: Avoidance of Revolution

Both academicians and prominent business leaders have devoted more than a few words to pointing out where Marx's predictions went awry. Much of this rhetoric has been ideological gloating, pure and simple. However, such a task can be a useful analytical step. Although I see no need to attempt even a brief formal critique of Marx, I will mention a few of the structural changes in capitalist societies which Marx did not anticipate as these observations will be helpful for later steps in our analysis.[2]

The first of these changes is frequently called the managerial revolution. The managerial revolution refers to the

---

[1] For a useful discussion of the various interpretations of the theory of misery, see T. Sowell, "Marx's 'Increasing Misery' Doctrine," *American Economic Review*, 1960, *50*, 111–120. Sowell tends to emphasize the difference between earlier and later works rather than contradictions in Marx's thinking. It seems to me that both occur, for in *Wage, Labour, and Capital*, which was first delivered as lectures during the same month that he and Engels wrote the *Manifesto*, his analysis tends to emphasize relative deprivation. What he seemed to be saying at that time was that the "most favorable situation" will be one of increasing relative deprivation while the most likely one will be increasing absolute deprivation. The works of Marx referred to in the above discussion may be found in K. Marx and F. Engels, *Selected Works*. (2 vols.)

[2] The comments which follow are primarily a summary of R. Dahrendorf's excellent discussion in his *Class and Class Conflict in Industrial Society*, 1959, pp. 41–67.

separation of formal ownership from actual control of large corporations. For the most part, these corporations are run and controlled by professional managers who own only infinitesimal amounts of the companies' stock. Because the stock of such companies is dispersed among so many individuals, even the largest stockholders are seldom successful in challenging the authority of these managers. The degree to which the legal owners of capital, namely, stockholders in corporations, have lost their power is still hotly debated, but this doubtless has been the long-term trend.[3] Marx anticipated at least aspects of this change in his discussion of joint-stock companies. A development which Marx did not anticipate was the increase in the education, skill, and specialization of the labor force. According to Marx, further industrialization would make the work force increasingly homogeneous and unskilled because the production process would become more and more standardized and simplified. Related to this upgrading of the labor force is a third development: the vast expansion of the white-collar middle class. A fourth development is the institutionalization of industrial conflict. The right of labor to organize and to bargain with management is now virtually undisputed. Moreover, a whole set of supplementary structures have been developed to assist in mediating conflicts of interest between labor and management.

Probably Marx's most problematical prediction was that the rich would get richer and the poor poorer—because as we have seen above, it is not clear what he meant. Quite clearly, the last half of the prediction is incorrect, at least in absolute terms, and probably in relative terms. There has been a definite trend of increasing levels of wealth for all social strata within industrial societies. But the picture is less clear in regard to the proportionate distribution of income and wealth, for example, whether the percentage of the national income going to the lowest tenth of the population is greater or less. Over the past one hundred years, income and wealth probably have become more equally distributed. However, it is by no means certain

[3] See G. Kolko, *Wealth and Power in America*, and W. Domhoff, *Who Rules America*, for arguments which stress the remaining power of large stockholders.

whether this trend continued into recent decades. In the United States, five points probably summarize the situation: (1) the income distribution before taxes has been virtually stable since World War II; (2) the current *effective* rate of taxes on reported income is very roughly the same for all levels of income—about 30 per cent; (3) transfer payments such as social security tend to redistribute income toward lower-income groups; (4) in all likelihood, the income of the wealthier groups is underreported; (5) no good data are available on the trends in distribution of wealth.[4] In short, although everybody is richer, and although equality is probably greater than when Marx wrote, the data do not enable us to identify a clear trend toward either greater equality or inequality. This same situation probably holds for most highly industrialized capitalist countries [5] although some, for example, Sweden, have explicit policies aimed at reducing income inequality.

The final structural change which we will consider is most central to the concerns of this study: the institutionalization of social mobility. Marx did not deny the possibility of social mobility; in fact his explanation of the lack of class formation in the United States hinges on social mobility.[6] But for Marx, the United States was a temporarily deviant case which would eventually follow suit through what he considered the basic processes of a capitalistic society. Yet not only have the rates of social mobility remained high in the United States, but high mobility characterizes most highly industrialized societies.

[4] The literature on distribution of income and wealth is extensive. Probably the best single source for the United States is H. P. Miller (see for example *Income Distribution in the United States*. For a radical perspective, see Kolko. For a sampling of recent economic research in this area, see L. Soltow (Ed.), *Six Papers on the Size and Distribution of Wealth and Income*. For an attempt to estimate the actual tax burdens of different income levels, see R. A. Herriot and H. P. Miller, "Who Paid the Taxes in 1968?"

[5] By capitalist countries I mean those in which large sectors of the economy are still privately owned and operated. Whether the welfare-state characteristic of non-Communist industrial societies is "really" capitalistic is an issue we need not resolve here.

[6] See *The Eighteenth Brumaire of Louis Bonaparte*, in Marx and Engels, p. 255.

Since the time of Marx, no successful revolutions of the left have taken place in a highly industrialized society. Moreover, on the whole, the level of class conflict seems to have diminished. Supposedly, the structural changes that we have just outlined are the major causes of the continued viability of non-Communist industrial societies. The last two changes discussed seem to be especially important. To quote Ralf Dahrendorf: "It was in particular the institutionalization of the two great social forces of mobility and equality that has steered the class structures and conflicts in directions unforeseen by Marx." [7]

Special Sanctification: American Social Stability

The previous section made the obvious point that capitalist societies have not collapsed as Marx predicted and identified some of the structural changes which are supposedly responsible for this outcome. But the changes outlined are characteristic of virtually all non-Communist industrial societies. Although no highly developed industrial society has undergone a revolution from the left, the extent of class conflict and political stability have varied considerably. Even compared with other industrialized Western democracies, America has tended to have low levels of class conflict, a low susceptibility to ideologies of the left, and a high degree of political stability. Let us now investigate some of the attempts to explain why, from among the redeemed, the United States has been particularly sanctified.

Conventional wisdom on this point is clear. Class conflict has been relatively low because the United States has traditionally been "the land of opportunity." [8] That is to say, it supposedly has high rates of social mobility. Furthermore, most of this mobility has been upward. This tremendous fluidity of our status structure is credited with preventing the formation of identifiable social classes and with dampening radical ideologies

[7] Dahrendorf, p. 57.
[8] This perspective originated with A. de Tocqueville and was probably true when he made his observations. The problem is that an initial observation and hypothesis became a convention. See his *Democracy in America*.

or political revolution. Of course, not even the conventional wisdom was committed to a uni-causal analysis, but traditionally, the primary explanation offered for our political stability has been "opportunity."

Understandably, studies which question or reject this traditional assumption have received considerable attention. The publication in 1959 of *Social Mobility in Industrial Society* by Seymour Martin Lipset and Reinhard Bendix was the first to cast serious doubt on the conventional explanation. When Lipset and Bendix compared the data then available for industrialized societies, they found that all had roughly comparable rates of social mobility. More precisely:

The data we have surveyed appear to indicate that mobility, as measured by movement across the manual-nonmanual dividing line, has been considerable in many countries of Western Europe as well as in the United States. Roughly comparable rates of mobility have been found under so many different social and economic conditions and in so many otherwise divergent samples that it may be more plausible to believe that the cause of mobility lies primarily in the economic expansion made possible by a given level of industrialization than to believe that it lies in the spasmodic dislocation of war and political upheaval. The overall finding certainly does not mean that there may not be important differences among countries which may be revealed once we have comparative studies of more detailed variations in occupational status. . . . But until such better evidence is available, it does entitle us to reject the banality that the societies of Western Europe are "static" but American society is "open." [9]

It follows that if the rates of social mobility have been the same for the United States and for other Western European countries, then social mobility, opportunity, and openness cannot be the explanation of the low levels of class conflict in the United States.

Lipset and Bendix suggest that one of the factors which

[9] Lipset and Bendix, p. 38.

explains our political stability is the cultural value attributed to mobility. According to their interpretation, social mobility will be viewed optimistically if perceived as the result of expanding opportunities in a politically stable society, but pessimistically if viewed as the consequences of two world wars and the turmoil caused by totalitarianism.

Cultural traditions, and especially cumulative political experience, may result, therefore, in a massive difference between the values that two different societies assign to social mobility and the effect that such values have on the social structure even though the actual proportion of mobile persons is the same in both. *Thus, where, as in the United States, social mobility receives positive encouragement, the existing opportunities for upward mobility probably help to sustain the acceptance of the social and political order by the lower classes. But such opportunities probably cannot shake the distrust of the prevailing order that exists among lower-class persons in such countries as France where the dominant historical image is one of an unfair distribution of opportunities in which little mobility occurs.*[10]

If this line of argument is accepted, we must explain why Americans have tended to perceive and interpret the social mobility they have experienced in terms "optimistic" enough to "sustain the acceptance of the social and political order." The primary explanation Lipset and Bendix offer for this optimism is what they call "ideological equalitarianism." Such an ideology does not deny differences in rank and authority, but emphasizes that the differences are temporary or accidental. This ideology has at least several manifestations. The first Lipset and Bendix call "equalitarianism of manners." In their casual day to day contacts Americans do not consider it good taste for those with high rank or authority to demand deferential attitude or behavior from those below them. According to Lipset and Bendix, this equalitarianism of manners is not only an ideal norm but is, for the most part, adhered to. The second manifestation of

[10] Lipset and Bendix, p. 77.

ideological equalitarianism is a tendency to give a materialistic interpretation to social differences. That is, "Americans frequently think of the differences of status and power, not as being what they really are, but rather as differences in the distribution of material goods." [11] Differences in material possessions are, in some sense, less alienating than differences in power, honor, and respect—in part because they are seen as temporary or accidental. A third manifestation is an emphasis on equality of opportunity—although inequalities may exist, everyone has a chance to gain higher rewards.

In sum, the argument is that political stability and, implicitly, lack of class conflict are due to an optimistic interpretation of social mobility and that this interpretation is, in turn, due to ideological equalitarianism.[12]

Since Lipset and Bendix completed their study, several new bodies of data have become available. Peter Blau and Otis Dudley Duncan have summarized these new findings and attempted to relate them to the conclusions of Lipset and Bendix.[13]

[11] Lipset and Bendix, p. 80.

[12] Actually, the Lipset and Bendix argument is considerably more complex than this. They mention six factors which supposedly contribute to political stability, an optimistic interpretation of mobility, and ideological equalitarianism. These factors are: (1) the absence of a feudal past; (2) the continuous high rate of social mobility; (3) the increase in educational opportunities; (4) the pattern of business careers; (5) the presence of immigrants and racial minorities; and (6) high levels of wealth and consumer goods. But the precise nature of the causal relationships suggested by Lipset and Bendix are unclear—at least to me. At some points, ideological equalitarianism seems to be an independent variable on a par with these other six factors. At other points, it seems to be an intervening variable between these six factors and the dependent variable of "optimism." However, some of these six variables seem to contribute directly to ideological equalitarianism (for instance, absence of a feudal past) while others (for instance, presence of immigrants and minorities) seem to have causal connections to "optimism" and political stability which do not pass through ideological equalitarianism. Such ambiguities in the causal model are to be expected in pioneering efforts, but they create confusion and have significance for later criticisms of Lipset and Bendix's work.

[13] See Blau and Duncan, *The American Occupational Structure*, pp. 432–441. Much of the data which Blau and Duncan compare was derived from S. M. Miller, "Comparative Social Mobility," *Current Sociology*, Vol. 9, 1960.

Blau and Duncan find that the new data confirms that there is "little difference among the various industrialized nations in the rate of occupational mobility between the blue-collar and the white-collar class." However, the United States does have "higher rates than most countries, corresponding to its advanced level of industrialization and education." [14] Moreover, the United States definitely has the highest rate of mobility from the working class into the elite classes. (The only other country with comparable mobility levels of this type is Puerto Rico.)

In light of these findings, Blau and Duncan suggest that the conclusions of Lipset and Bendix need revision. First, they question whether ideological equalitarianism is an adequate explanation of American optimism and stability. According to Blau and Duncan, "One does not have to be an orthodox Marxist to accept the proposition that ideologies and social values are rooted in existential conditions of the social structure." [15] Consequently, an explanation based on ideological equalitarianism "begs the question of why Americans continue to believe that class differences merely indicate differences in material advantages and rewards that are accessible to all, whereas men in other societies do not, if the actual chances of men from lower strata to achieve superior class position are no better in the United States than in other industrial nations." [16] According to Blau and Duncan, the inconsistencies are explained by their findings that in the United States, men from the lower strata have greater opportunities to move into the elite strata than do men in other societies. Although the rates of mobility between the white-collar and blue-collar strata may be the same for most industrial countries, the United States has significantly greater opportunities for *long distance* upward mobility. According to Blau and Duncan, this mobility sustains an ideology which both

[14] Blau and Duncan, p. 433.
[15] Blau and Duncan, p. 436–437.
[16] Blau and Duncan, p. 437.
This criticism is not fair to Lipset and Bendix because, as I indicated in an earlier footnote, they suggest several structural factors which reinforce the equalitarian ideology although admittedly their argument lacks clarity at this point.

recognizes and *significantly exaggerates* these superior opportunities.

Blau and Duncan go on to argue that, along with the partly real and partly exaggerated belief in greater opportunities, two other factors have contributed to political stability in the United States. The first is the widely noted emphasis on materialism. They agree with the implication by Lipset and Bendix that materialism, combined with the ideology of opportunity, helps reduce patterns of deference and social subordination that tend to develop in status systems not emphasizing material possessions. The emphasis on material possessions supposedly deemphasizes ascribed traits and therefore emphasizes characteristics which can be earned rather than simply assigned at birth. Such an emphasis also makes translating economic achievements into other forms of status easier. Both of these factors tend to make status differences impermanent and by implication changeable. Whatever deference is received by those with high rank must be bought with money or earned by demonstrations of superior competence—rather than inherited through ascribed statuses.

The second factor which contributes to stability is a high standard of living. The high standard of living is in part a result of the emphasis on material goods; where such goods are highly valued, both as a sign of social status and in their own right, considerable effort will be devoted to producing such goods. Consequent increases in the standard of living have two significant effects in this context. First, consumer goods will tend to become more equally distributed, and therefore some of the class differences in life style will be reduced. Second, most individuals will experience significant improvements in their absolute economic condition which is all the more appreciated where there is a strong emphasis on the value of material goods. Blau and Duncan conclude:

The stability of American democracy is undoubtedly related to superior chances of upward mobility in this country, its high standard of living, and the low degree of status deference between social strata. For these conditions make it unlikely that

*large numbers of underprivileged men experience oppression,
despair of all hope, and become so disaffected with the existing
system of differential rewards as well as with political institutions
that they join extremist political movements committed to violent rebellion.*[17]

Not unexpectedly, Blau and Duncan's revisions of the
Lipset-Bendix thesis have not been universally accepted. T. B.
Bottomore writes:

*I do not find this [higher rate of long-range mobility as an ex-
planation of the continued American faith in the equalitarian
ideology] any more convincing than the Lipset-Bendix thesis.
There was a fairly long period, from the 1880s to the end of
the Progressive Era, when the American ideology was strongly
challenged and rejected by historians and sociologists and by a
substantial part of the population. What we have to explain is
how it came to be reestablished. A major influence, in my view,
was the failure of the radical and protest movements to establish themselves as an opposition party, and this in turn was
affected by the ethnic diversity of the population and the lack
of common traditions resulting from mass immigration, by the
peculiar situation of the Negroes, and eventually by the steadily
rising levels of living. The marginally higher rate of long-range
mobility, even if it is a fact, seems to me a minor factor. On the
other hand, the ideology itself must have had some effect; it
possessed an inherent force, and after 1918, there was nothing
coherent to challenge it. But, it does not follow that in the
1960s we must assume that this pre-Civil War ideology will
persist or will be so influential. Negroes and students, at least,
are already rejecting it.*[18]

Devoting pages to explanations of political stability (and
low levels of class conflict) may seem like a sick joke. In the
last half of the 1960s, what required explanation was not stabil-

[17] Blau and Duncan, p. 439.
[18] T. B. Bottomore, *American Sociological Review*, 1968, *33*, 295–
296.

ity but instability, not harmony but conflict. We will return to the problem of explaining America's political stability in the first half of the twentieth century, but for the moment, let us turn to the problems of our more recent history.

The Fall from Grace: Conflict Groups

I do not think it will be necessary to detail the social conflict of the 1960s. The outline is familiar; the central issues were the war in Indochina, campus unrest, racial inequality, and to a lesser extent women's rights. But if a history of these conflicts is not needed, we will need (for later stages of the analysis) to identify in a more precise way the actors who have been involved in these conflicts.

In the first chapter of this book, I suggested that endless striving was an important contributing factor in many of our current social problems. Implicit in that discussion was my distinction between two levels or types of social pathologies. The first were those which affect virtually all the population—for example, pollution. Second were social irritants which primarily affected a particular subpopulation—for instance, racial discrimination. I now wish to focus on this second level: group conflict.

Since the mid-1960s, the major cleavages in American society have been between those groups I have labelled the excluded, the vulnerable, and the chosen. Most of the conflict has pitted the vulnerable against one or both of the other groups. Consequently, an investigation of the causes of conflict and instability in the United States requires an explanation of the conflict between these groups. But before such an analysis can begin, we must elaborate on the nature of these three groups.

Each of these conflict groups has at least three relevant levels. First, they are social aggregates, namely, a category of individuals who share a set of social traits in common (for instance race). Second, they contain collectivities, namely, social aggregates in which the individuals have come to share a degree of mutual awareness and common identity. Third, they contain networks of organizations, namely, sets of formal organizations whose members are drawn primarily from a particular collectivity and whose primary function is to advance the interest of that collectivity. Obviously, the first level (aggregates) includes more individuals than the second level (collectivities), and this level is more inclusive than the third level (organizations).[19] I make this distinction in order to stress that not all individuals in a particular social category necessarily identify with the parallel collectivity, hold membership in the parallel organizations, or actively participate in the conflicts between this group and others. There is an assumption, however, that each of these categories is an identifiable entity with a significant degree of cohesiveness and organization.

Next, we must clarify the nature of the traits which the members of each group have in common. Early in this century, the famous German sociologist, Max Weber, drew a distinction between classes, status groups, and parties.[20] "Party" means just about what "political party" means in everyday usage. "Class" refers to divisions based upon economic differences. "Status groups" are based upon common levels (positive or negative) of social prestige, honor, or respectability, which in turn can be connected with any quality the members of the group share in common.[21] Weber emphasized that these three types of social divisions could be related to one another in a variety of ways. "Honor" might be tied to economic position but frequently is not. A political party might be based primarily upon a particular class or status group or might cut across several such groups.

In Weber's terms, the conflict groups that I have identified—the excluded, the chosen, and the vulnerable—are pri-

[19] These distinctions are loosely borrowed from Amitai Etzioni (*The Active Society*) and have a number of contemporary parallels (for instance, Dahrendorf's distinction between quasigroups, interest groups, and conflict groups, p. 173), and historical precedents (for instance, Marx's distinction between "a class in itself" and "a class for itself").

[20] Max Weber, "Class, Status, and Party," 1946. The summary of Weber's definitions presented here simplifies considerably his subtle and complex discussion.

[21] For a note on the difficulties inherent in Weber's concept of status groups, see Max Weber, *The Theory of Social and Economic Organization*, 1947, pp. 347, 428–429.

marily status groups. The trait which the excluded have in common is that they are discriminated against on the basis of some highly visible ascribed characteristic—for instance, race, sex, or language. Blacks, women, and Chicanos are often treated as inferior or less honorable than white males with the same levels of qualification. Moreover, this discrimination is permanent throughout the individual's lifetime; no amount of training, maturity, or seniority removes the dishonor—although it may help to reduce it. These groups demand that their particular identifying characteristic, for example blackness, be given the same honor and privileges as the identifying characteristics of the dominant group. From a historical perspective, this is a continuation of the battles against inherited privileges begun with the bourgeois revolutions of the eighteenth and nineteenth centuries.

The characteristic common to the chosen is their potential membership in the establishment—even in its elite. Yet, they are relegated to a position of dependency during their preparation. They are not yet full participants in the economic system and are considered dependents either of their parents or of charitable institutions—the scholarship and loan programs of governments, foundations, and colleges. Dependency produces an accompanying inferiority and subordination—at least implicitly. Most of the chosen are both young and students and are looked upon as dependent and inferior. However, either one of these attributes—being young or being a student—is a sufficient condition to being categorized as a dependent. Graduate students thirty and forty years old are viewed as less-than-mature adults.[22] On the other hand, those under twenty-one frequently have been treated as dependents even if they were not students and irrespective of their economic or marital status.

The vulnerable are characterized by their full membership in "the system." They are mature, white, "productive" members of society. This full membership is to the social and economic

[22] For example, being a student sometimes bars a person from obtaining credit. During my own years as a graduate student, I was twice denied credit simply because I was a student. The creditors refused to investigate either my sources of income or my credit rating.

sectors what citizenship is to the political sector. Certainly not all full members (or citizens) are equal with respect to wealth, power, and so on. But they do receive a type of basic honor and respect that is not accorded to the excluded and the chosen.

To describe the excluded, the chosen, and the vulnerable as status groups is not to deny the important economic dimensions of these divisions. The concepts of class and status groups should not be treated as absolute distinctions but as analytical models or ideal-type constructs, to use Weber's own language. Concrete historical groupings approximate these models. My argument is that the three groups that I have identified and discussed come closer to Weber's ideal-type model of a status group than the model of a social class. The defining characteristic of each of these groups is not their economic position but a status characteristic. Later, I will argue that the formation and activation of these conflict groups is very definitely related—in a complex way—to economic inequalities. It is important, however, not to confuse antecedent causes of a social grouping with the defining characteristic of that unit. In my judgment, the distinctive characteristic of each group is more a matter of honor than of economics.

One final point about the nature of these conflict groups: there is great variation within each group. This variation is especially true for the vulnerable which includes the bulk of the American population. The differences in power and wealth within this group are enormous. Nonetheless, for the purposes of analysis, we treat them as a single conflict group because in recent years, the most bitter conflicts in our society have centered on struggles with this group rather than within it.

The Effect of Status
Inflation and
Education on Levels
of Social Conflict

Eight

I will now try to throw some light on the factors which have helped to produce and activate the conflict groups described above. However, I first want to undertake an even more presumptuous task and attempt to tie together, in one explanation, the low levels of conflict in earlier years and the high levels of conflict in recent years. Actually, explanation is too strong a word. More accurately, I hope to identify and describe social processes which have been important contributing factors first to stability and then to conflict. As those with only modest amounts of clairvoyance may have anticipated, the interpretation will center on status inflation and the expansion of education.

Since Hegel and Marx, the idea of dialectical change has been a standard conceptual tool—some would say gimmick—of academicians. The basic notion of dialectic change is that within any idea or social process (thesis) there is a contradiction (antithesis) that becomes increasingly manifest as the initial trend or idea is elaborated. The thesis and the antithesis come into conflict and are eventually merged into a new synthesis. If frequency of mention were a measure of truth, this conceptual scheme would probably have to be declared the most certain hypothesis in social theory. Too often, however, this mode of analysis remains on such a high level of abstraction that the exact nature of the contradiction and the specific processes which produce the conflict and change of direction are not clear. Despite this danger, this traditional scheme seems useful in organizing the analysis which follows.

The basic argument is simple: from approximately 1900 to 1960, the expansion of educational opportunities has contributed significantly to the lack of class conflict and to political stability in general; since that time the continuing expansion of (higher) education has contributed significantly to the social conflict.[1]

Schooling and Stability

Let us begin by briefly recalling the various explanations that have been offered for America's political stability. Conventional wisdom attributed the stability primarily to greater

[1] For an analysis which has a number of points in common with the one which follows, see R. Flacks, "The Roots of Student Protest," *The Journal of Social Issues*, 1967, 23, 52–75.

opportunity, namely, high rates of social mobility. Seymour Lipset and Reinhard Bendix call this wisdom into serious question by their findings that most industrialized societies have rates of mobility that are virtually as high as those for the United States. They explain our greater stability in terms of the optimistic view Americans have of their experience in the stratification structure; because the United States never experienced the inequalities of feudalism, there has always been a strong ideological equalitarianism which mitigated inequalities and exaggerated actual opportunities. Peter Blau and Otis Duncan criticize this explanation on the grounds that ideologies are not self-sustaining and that they must be based upon "existential conditions of the social structure." According to them, the existential condition which has sustained this ideology is the higher rate of long-range mobility from the lower classes into the elite; this type of mobility is considerably greater in the United States than in other industrial societies. T. B. Bottomore finds this explanation unconvincing and notes that during the Progressive period, ideological equalitarianism was rejected by many so that an explanation of how it was reestablished is necessary.

Bottomore is correct in pointing out that the ideology of equal opportunity came under serious attack in the last two decades of the nineteenth century and was rejected by "a substantial part of the population." But even then, equalitarianism was still the dominant ideology. (Just as it has been the dominant view in recent years even though under serious attack.) The problem, then, is to explain how this dominant traditional ideology fought off its attackers and reestablished itself.

I stress this point not because I wish to quibble with Bottomore's language but because the structural factors and events which are required to bring about the reestablishment of a questioned ideology are considerably less monumental than the factors necessary to establish a new ideology or reestablish a rejected one.

Undoubtedly, the factors which brought about the relegitimation of this ideology are manifold. For example, antitrust and civil-service legislation were probably important; continued

economic expansion was a factor; and ethnic divisions and immigration undoubtedly played a role in reducing the effectiveness of class-based protest movements. I would like, however,
to suggest as a tentative hypothesis that the expansion of secondary education played an important, possibly crucial, role.

Although the expansion of secondary education began
during the Progressive era, significant percentages of the population were unaffected until after World War I. Through 1880,
only a little over 1 per cent of the precollege student population were enrolled in secondary school. By 1900, the figure
had jumped to 3.3 per cent. From that time until 1920, the
percentage of students in secondary education almost doubled
each decade. Increases almost as large were experienced from
1920 until 1940 when the percentage of students in secondary
education reached 26 per cent. The percentage has remained
relatively constant since that time. Virtually the same growth
pattern is evident if the percentage of the school-age population (rather than the percentage of enrolled students) attending
high school is the basis of comparison. These figures may not
be particularly impressive unless they are viewed in relation to
primary-school enrollments. During this same period, 1880–
1940, the percentage of school-age children (five- through
seventeen-year olds) attending primary school remained virtually the same. In other words, the scope and social visibility
of primary schooling remained about constant—it was already
nearly universal—while the scope of secondary education increased over twenty-five times.[2]

The objection may be made that to stress an increase of
"over twenty-five times" is misleading since it is due to the very
low percentage of secondary students enrolled in the early years

[2] These statistics are taken or derived from US Office of Education, *Digest of Educational Statistics, 1969*, Table 30. Although there is
some question whether these statistics are a reliable indicator of the
absolute level of enrollments at any given time, they do probably give
a reasonably accurate picture of the historical trend. For a useful note
on the problems inherent in these statistics, see R. Welter, *Popular Education and Democratic Thought in America, 1962*, p. 378, fn. 24. However, the statistics now available may be slightly more reliable than
when Welter wrote.

of the period. (For example, if instead of 1880, we take 1900 as a base, when the percentage of students in secondary education was only 3.3, the scope of the secondary system increased only eight times by 1940, rather than "25 times." But the expansion of the social visibility of secondary education is precisely the point. This visible expansion of educational opportunities may have played a significant role in maintaining "ideological equalitarianism"—even if it only produced negligible effects on social mobility or equality of opportunity.

The visibility of a positively valued social development may increase the optimism of those who are not directly affected as well as those who are. For example, at the same time a housing shortage may exist on the collective level, many individuals may have adequate housing. If one of these individuals sees many new apartment buildings going up in his neighborhood, he may get the impression that the housing shortage is being solved, even if he continues to live in the same place. The expansion of the educational system may have a similar effect on those who have no direct connection with this system, particularly older persons.

This supposedly social visible expansion of the school system was, however, accompanied by a definite increase in the percentage of the population that experienced upward educational mobility. For example, of the men who were approximately seventeen during the period from 1915 to 1924, 47 per cent had more education than their fathers whereas 11 per cent had less. In contrast, of those men who were seventeen between 1935 and 1944, 62 per cent had more education than their fathers whereas 7 per cent had less. Stated slightly differently, in the earlier period, a majority of the male population, 53 per cent, had either the same or less education than their fathers whereas in the later period, a large majority—approaching two-thirds—of the male population had experienced upward educational mobility.[3] The importance of this significant but modest

[3] These figures are taken from W. Spady, "Educational Mobility and Access: Growth and Paradoxes," *American Journal of Sociology,* 1967, 73, 275, Table 1.

increase in upward educational mobility should not be over-stated. Roughly parallel increases in occupational mobility were being experienced during the same period.[4] However, there are several reasons that educational mobility may be more important in maintaining an equalitarian ideology than occupational mobility or even increases in the standard of living. First, educational mobility is probably more discernible than occupational mobility or changes in the standard of living. There are socially standardized measures of educational attainment—the number of years of schooling, diplomas, degrees, and so on. In contrast, occupational prestige is more ambiguous. Does the factory worker or even the skilled construction worker who grew up on a farm owned and operated by his father feel that his occupational status is significantly higher than his father's? Probably not. But it is clear to him that his high school diploma is a significant step up from his father's seven or eight years of schooling.

There may also be a tendency to discount the social value of increases in income at a faster rate than increases in education. "A dollar is not worth what it used to be," or "It is always hard to make ends meet," are common expressions. On the other hand, comments to the effect that high school diplomas or college degrees are worth less than they once were seem to occur less frequently. Once again, however, the significance of such a process—if it exists at all—should not be overemphasized, but that such perceptions increase the social significance of upward educational mobility is at least plausible.

My second main point concerning upward educational mobility is that we may be overlooking the social group on which its stabilizing effect may be greatest: parents. We generally assume that the primary effect of social mobility is on sons and daughters who experience an improvement in their social position or standard of living. But the most important effect may be upon the parents. Parents obviously gain great satisfaction from the achievements of their children. In some

[4] See O. Duncan, "The Trend of Occupational Mobility in the United States," *American Sociological Review*, 1965, *30*, 491–498.

situations, this type of satisfaction may be more important in maintaining people's commitment to a particular social order than the parents' own opportunities for a higher social status or standard of living. It may be difficult for parents to have a clear idea of their children's long-term chances for occupational and economic advancement. In contrast, they will have fairly early in their own life cycle a pretty clear picture of the educational opportunities that will be available to their children. If it seems reasonably clear that their children will have a chance to "improve themselves," this opportunity may go a long way in mitigating whatever personal frustrations the parents may experience in the stratification system.

Up to this point, I have argued that the expansion of secondary education contributed to the reestablishment and maintenance of ideological equalitarianism in two ways. First, the expansion of the secondary school system itself probably had significant social visibility, which in turn contributed to the belief that there were significant and increasing opportunities for social and educational mobility. Second, this expansion of secondary schools was in fact followed by high and increasing rates of upward educational mobility, or parents' anticipation of it for their children (or both), which contributed to the maintenance of the ideology of opportunity.

But these two social processes are not the most direct, nor possibly the most important, effect of expanded secondary education on this ideology. The most direct effect comes through what the schools teach their students. I am not versed in the history of American educational curriculum, but I am reasonably sure that most schools in America have devoted considerable effort to inculcating into the student what we have been calling the "ideology of opportunity" or "ideological equalitarianism."

This process is probably especially significant at the secondary level for a number of reasons. First, until about secondary-school age, students are limited in their ability to deal with such ideologies in an intellectual fashion. Second, during the first half of the twentieth century, secondary schools increasingly served as the transitional phase between economic dependence upon parents and adult participation in the economic and social structure. Consequently, secondary students probably had a relatively high interest in the ideologies that purported to explain how rewards were allocated in the real world of adulthood. Third, significant amounts of these ideologies are included in the formal curriculum of secondary schools in the form of courses in civics and history. Finally, the widespread institution of secondary education gave children up to four additional years of ideological indoctrination.

The argument up to now has focused on how the expansion of the education system contributed to the ideology of mobility and opportunity, not on how it might have influenced occupational mobility directly. In Part II we found no evidence that the expansion of the education system had significantly *increased* the level of equality of opportunity. However, this expansion probably has been a significant factor in *maintaining* the degree of equality of opportunity that we have experienced since World War I.

Moreover, if educational expansion has not increased equality of opportunity, it seemingly has contributed to the increases in (structural) upward occupational mobility. Education may not have given the poor man's son the same chance as a rich man's son, but he has a "better" job than his father had. He is much more likely to have a white-collar job than his father because there are both absolutely and proportionately many more white-collar jobs.

This change was accomplished on the supply side of the labor market by giving individuals the educational skills they supposedly needed to move up. But probably of greater significance is the effect that an expanding educational sector has on the demand side, that is, on the number of new high-status jobs being created. At least four social processes have been at work here. Probably most important is the effect of postponing entry into the work force; having young men spend additional years in school means that at any given time, the competition for the available jobs is reduced. Second, a number of jobs, mainly in teaching, are created by expanding the education system. In 1920, the first year for which data are available, there were 678,000 staff members in elementary and secondary schools. This number constituted about 0.6 per cent of the total population. By 1940, the figure had increased to about 0.7 per cent. By 1965, the figure was 0.9 per cent, which represented 1,885,-000 professional jobs.[5] Third is the effect on fertility. Higher levels of education are associated with high occupational status and with low birth rates. Consequently, education has been partly responsible for higher-status groups producing "less than their share" of the next generation. This reduction has contributed to the number of vacancies available at the upper end of the occupational structure. Evidence indicates, however, that the effect of education on reducing fertility is diminishing.[6] Finally, the expansion of education has contributed to the maintenance of equality of opportunity, which has, in turn, contributed to the number of upper-level jobs available to individuals of low-status origins. This mobility occurs because equality of opportunity means, by definition, that many of the sons of high-status fathers will be downwardly mobile, at least in relative terms, although not necessarily in absolute terms. To repeat an earlier example, the sons may have higher levels of absolute income than their fathers, but the sons will be lower in the income distribution of their own generation than their fathers were in their generation. Therefore, in the son's generation, there will be high-status jobs available to those of low-status origins.

At the risk of repetitiveness, let me summarize the rather complicated line of argument. The reestablishment and maintenance of ideological equalitarianism was at least in part due to what was probably a highly visible expansion of secondary education. This expansion contributed to upward educational mobility, which is probably of special significance because this type of mobility is easy to see and measure and provides satisfactions to parents and children. The expansion of secondary schools also provided important additional opportunities for

[5] Data derived from US Office of Education, *Digest of Educational Statistics,* 1969, Table 30.

[6] See P. Blau and O. D. Duncan, *The American Occupational Structure,* 1967, pp. 363–365.

direct indoctrination of the traditional ideology. All of these processes could have helped to maintain ideological equalitarianism without having any effect in the occupational and economic structures as such. But expanded education probably did increase (structural) upward occupational mobility by affecting the supply of trained workers and especially by increasing demand through delaying entry into the job market, creating teaching jobs, and lowering fertility. Finally, the expansion of education probably operated through the mechanism that is usually assumed to be its primary effect—by helping to maintain, if not increase, past levels of equality of opportunity. If the expansion of secondary education did not significantly increase equality of opportunity, it did play an important role in providing an optimistic and positive social interpretation to the mobility and opportunity that was in fact experienced. And, according to the Lipset-Bendix thesis, this positive social interpretation in turn contributed to the reduction of social conflict and the maintenance of political stability.

Schooling and Conflict

The thesis of this section is that the expansion of education, primarily higher education, since World War II has set in motion a number of social processes which have caused students and young people to question the legitimacy of the American social structure and ideology in general and ideological equalitarianism in particular.

This questioning has not caused the processes which are discussed in the previous section—as contributing factors to social stability—to cease to operate. But at least some of these processes have diminished considerably, for instance, the effect of education in reducing fertility or the more chauvinistic types of ideological instruction. More important, whatever stabilizing effects these processes continue to have seem to be increasingly negated by new social processes which have evolved from the continued expansion of education. We now turn to the task of identifying some of these processes.

One significant difference between the secondary-education system and the higher-education system is the content of the ideologies to which students are exposed. In the better colleges and universities, the professors are not only teachers, but also—in many cases primarily—professional scholars and intellectuals. Compared with most other social categories, this group tends to be less provincial, more relativistic in their values, and more inclined to be suspicious of traditional ideologies. Moreover, because of the traditions and structure of higher education, professors tend to have much more academic freedom than lower-level teachers. As a result of these factors, they have tended to be significantly more critical of the status quo and the supporting ideologies than most secondary teachers. I am not arguing that most college professors are wild-eyed radicals, intent on leading their students to revolution. Traditionally, the majority have been liberal Democrats. However, to the extent that there were any vocal radicals in our society, they have often been academicians. This tendency of college professors to criticize traditional ideologies and espouse those which are considerably to the left of those most frequently encountered in high schools does not establish the fact that their students adopt these ideologies. But the burden of proof is on those who argue against the liberalizing influences of higher education.[7] Moreover, in all likelihood, these influences are related to the ideologies they encounter among their professors. What we have said about teachers also holds for the contrast between high school and college books and curriculum materials.

Let me summarize. The exposure of an increasing percentage of young people to the curriculum, formal and informal, of secondary schools during the period between World War I and World War II helped to reinforce and maintain the traditional ideologies. Since World War II, the exposure of greater and greater numbers to higher education has contributed to the erosion of these ideologies.

The second process which has caused the expansion of education to result in conflict rather than stability is the tendency

---

[7] Actually, a good deal of empirical research does indicate that higher education has a liberalizing effect on the students' social and political attitudes. (See K. Feldman and T. Newcomb, *The Impact of College*, 1969.)

for students to become alienated from the educational process itself. At least two broad subprocesses are involved here. The first can be summed up in the phrase *the bureaucratization of education*. As the education system has become larger and larger, it has tended to resort to various types of bureaucratic control and processing in order to cope with the administrative problems of providing education to so many. This tendency has been further aggravated by a decline in the effectiveness of the traditional and more informal methods of social control that were typical of an earlier period. Even in primary schools, and certainly in high schools and colleges, teachers seldom are acquainted with their students' families. Teachers can no longer easily bring family pressure to bear on an academic or disciplinary problem. Formal and legal controls, for example, probation and suspension, have been instituted. In college, the large lecture section in which the student has little or no contact with the main instructor is a common experience and a common complaint among students. The introduction of computerized data processing has virtually turned the college student into a number, at least insofar as most official records are concerned. A corollary is that most communications between the student and the officials of his school are via form letter printed by computer. Whether bureaucratization of this type is always alienating remains an open question. That it has been alienating to many students seems clear.

The second subprocess which adds to alienation from the educational process is dissatisfaction with the curriculum. Students constantly complain about the irrelevance of the subject matter they are required to study. There is certainly objective basis to this complaint.[8] Colleges and universities, and especially their faculties, are notoriously conservative when it comes to restructuring their own institutions. However, they are probably

---

[8] See for example I. Berg, *Education and Jobs: The Great Training Robbery* (New York: Praeger, 1970). Berg finds that employers frequently require educational credentials that have little or nothing to do with actual job requirements. Of course, this gap between the training required and the work to be done is only one aspect of the issue of irrelevancy.

no more recalcitrant now than in the past. In this connection, we need to remember that educational relevancy is not a new issue; it is a perennial one. But whether or not college curricula are actually less relevant than in the past, students apparently think they are and this adds to their alienation.

The third broad subprocess which contributes to alienation in the educational process is the increased number of years the student must remain in school. Students who seek college degrees, not to speak of graduate degrees, are relegated to the status of student well into their adult life. As noted earlier, the student is usually in a position of dependence and consequently subordination. Bennett Berger [9] has referred to the lengthening of this period of dependence and subordination as the "juvenilization" of our youth. Three things probably accentuate the alienating effect of the trend toward extending the period of subordination. First, as indicated earlier, the period of subordination occurs at a time when the instructional process itself brings to the student's attention criticisms of the traditional ideologies used to legitimize subordination and inequality. Second, because of their superior levels of education, students not infrequently perceive themselves as more informed and more qualified to exercise influence and responsibility than many individuals in the "adult" world. Third, this juvenilization has occurred during a historical era experiencing steady erosion of the legitimacy of asymmetrical forms of authority.[10] The expansion of education has probably contributed to this broader trend, although it is only one of many contributing factors.

Thus far, we have focused on the alienating effects that more years of schooling have on individuals at the level of higher education. But it is also likely that increasing the average number of years of schooling has negative consequences at the secondary level. At least two mechanisms are involved. The higher the average level of education, the lower the prestige derived from lower levels of schooling, that is, inflation occurs.

[9] B. Berger, "The New Stage of American Man—Almost Endless Adolescence," *The New York Times Magazine*, November 2, 1969.
[10] See W. Metzger, "The Crisis of Academic Authority," *Daedalus*, 1970, *99*, 568–608.

This inflation probably means that high school students receive fewer positive sanctions for their participation in secondary education than did earlier generations. Parents and friends no longer "carry on" over someone because he is in high school or even college. Middle- and upper-class students must now go on to graduate school before much note is taken of their educational progress. On the other hand, negative sanctions are meted out if the student is not progressing satisfactorily through the lower stages of the schooling system. To be sure, lower-level students receive positive reinforcement for their efforts, but structural changes in the system—the addition of a higher layer—makes it probable that they now receive more negative sanctions and fewer positive sanctions than earlier generations.[11] If the earlier stages of the educational process are more alienating, the effects of frustration experienced in the later stages of schooling are likely to be magnified in an increasingly cumulative and negative effect.

The second factor which may increase alienation at the lower levels of schooling is the increased emphasis on preparation for college. The pressure on high school students to do well on their college boards is a much discussed topic. This pressure has doubtlessly raised the anxiety level of many high school students and has probably contributed to their feelings of alienation.

To summarize this section: The content of higher education has a tendency to undercut rather than support traditional ideologies, whereas primary and secondary education has tended to support these ideologies. The expansion of educational opportunities has introduced processes which tend to alienate students from the educational process itself.

I now want to suggest that there are at least theoretical reasons that the expansion of opportunities for higher education may increase status anxiety for students from high-status backgrounds and lead them to identify with radical ideologies. Since

[11] For an interesting discussion which has at least indirect relevance to this process, see T. D. Kemper, "Reference Groups, Socialization, and Achievement," *American Sociological Review*, 1965, *33*, 31–45.

Richard Hofstadter suggested that the leadership of the Progressive movement might be understood in terms of threatened loss of social status, considerable literature has developed on "status politics." [12] To oversimplify things considerably, threatened or actual losses in social status make people open to radical ideologies.

One of the notable characteristics of the radical student movement is that many students have been drawn from relatively high-status backgrounds. In most cases, these students have above-average academic ability. Consequently, it appears that there is little chance of their being threatened with a loss of social status because they have both the resources and the ability to secure the educational credentials needed to maintain their superior status position. This, of course, was one of the main arguments offered in Part II as to why expanded opportunities for higher education were not likely to increase equality of opportunity. But although upper-class students will generally be able to maintain their high social status through educational achievement, the process creates significant levels of anxiety. Educational achievement is bound to be considerably more anxiety producing than earlier forms of transmitting status from parents to children; the likelihood that most from high-status origins will succeed via education is not the same thing as virtual certainty that *you* will succeed via inheritance. Moreover, maintaining high status through educational achievements involves considerable cost in time, money and effort (physical, intellectual, and psychic). The more the educational ladder is extended, the greater these are. The fact that one is able to pay these costs does not mean that one enjoys doing so. For the upper-class student must invest heavily in extended higher education simply to stay where he is. He has the choice of paying the cost and gaining nothing or not paying the cost and losing a great deal. It seems reasonable that he would have an affinity for ideologies which attack this system of status allocation. On

[12] R. Hofstadter, *The Age of Reform*, 1956, Chap. 4. See also D. Bell (Ed.), *The Radical Right*, 1963, and J. R. Gusfield, *Symbolic Crusade*, 1966.

the surface, these students would appear more open to ideologies of the right than the left. But most are in fact adherents of the ideology of equality of opportunity—at least they reject the notion that social status should be allocated according to inherited ascribed characteristics. To accept a rightist ideology would go against both the liberal to radical perspectives they have been exposed to in college and the traditional ideological equalitarianism that they were taught earlier. On the other hand, ideologies which espouse a radical equalitarianism rather than equality of opportunity, at least project a system in which there would be no status anxiety and no possibility of having low status. All would be equal and no one would feel a need for extended education (with its high costs) simply in order to avoid loss of status. Such a sociopsychological process operates for the most part on a subconscious, or at least nonverbalized level. Nonetheless, such an interpretation helps to identify some of the self interests which motivate radicals from high-status origins. Consequently, we do not have to explain their behavior strictly in terms of the university's ability to inculcate ideologies which are contrary to their self-interest nor resort to strained arguments that all students are members of the working class.

So far, we have considered factors which undercut the traditional ideologies or which contribute to the personal alienation of the student. Now I want to suggest how the expansion of educational opportunities has also provided a structural base for the development of a deviant subculture and a protest movement.

The mechanisms at work here are fairly obvious. The expansion of schooling has been paralleled by an increase in the significance of peer relationships while relationships with the family and other aspects of the adult world have been diminished. The historical trend in US education has involved not only additional years in school but also a steady increase in the length of the school year and the regularity of attendance. In 1900, the average number of days attended by each pupil enrolled was 99; in 1965 the average was 164.[13] Extracurricular activities have

[13] US Office of Education, *Digest of Educational Statistics, 1969*, Table 30.

increased significantly the length of the school day for many secondary students. In addition to the factors related to schooling as such, automobiles and telephones have greatly facilitated the strengthening of peer-group relationships.

The expansion of higher education has added several important additional factors. The most important factor is the change in residential patterns. In college, most students not only spend their days together, but they live with one another in their own community. Whatever contacts they have had with adults are drastically reduced. This reduction probably holds for all types of adult relationships but especially for daily interaction in intimate primary relationships, such as those in the family. As a result of this and other factors suggested earlier, there is a great reduction in effective social control by adults. Occasionally, colleges still attempt to maintain various types of *in loco parentis* control, but they are having less and less success and even the formalities are being abandoned. Finally, college students, especially graduate students, have levels of knowledge, skill, and experience that secondary students do not. This knowledge greatly increases their effectiveness in organizing articulate protests.

So we see that inherent in the expansion of the education system are processes which contribute to (1) alienation from traditional structures and ideologies; (2) the development of alternative ideologies; (3) a structural basis for a deviant subculture; and (4) the skills to organize that subculture into an effective protest group.

Up to this point, I have avoided introducing *ad hoc* variables into the analysis. That is, all of the factors mentioned above have been more or less directly related to the expansion of education.[14] However, a number of factors and events not directly related to educational expansion have obviously contributed to the emergence of students as a major conflict group in our society. I want to mention three of these factors and suggest their relationship to the processes already described.

[14] The only exceptions have been the mention of the effect that automobiles and telephones have had on peer relations, and the general decrease in the legitimacy of assymetrical authority relationships.

First, new levels of affluence are transforming basic values and motivations. Contemporary theorists from Maslow to Galbraith have suggested a hierarchy or sequence of needs; as societies evolve their needs, their basis of power and their motivational focus change. For example, Galbraith argues:

Power in economic life has over time passed from the ancient association with land to association with capital and then on, in recent times, to the composite of knowledge and skills [associated with the economic elite of industrial society]. . . . There have been associated shifts in the motivations to which men respond. Compulsion had an ancient association with land. Pecuniary motivation had a similar association with capital. Identification and adaptation are associated with [highly industrial societies].[15]

If such ideas are correct, the greatest changes have probably come to those who were socialized after World War II—primarily the students of recent years. When a tendency toward new basic values due to new affluence is combined with the educational processes described, the two factors most likely reinforce each other.

The second notion is that new patterns of permissive child rearing have reduced this generation's respect for authority and motivation for achievement. Once again, to the extent that it is true it would reinforce the alienating processes of the educational system, and vice versa.

These two factors along with the expansion of education have combined to produce a latent conflict group. But in addition, critical historical events have played a crucial role in transforming this latent conflict group into an active protest movement. The first event is the emergence of the civil rights movement. The civil rights movement greatly increased students' awareness of the social injustices that exist in our society and reduced the credibility of ideological equalitarianism. Finally,

[15] J. K. Galbraith, *The New Industrial State*, 1968, p. 150. I cite this particular evolutionary theory not because it directly explains the new values of the younger generation but because it clearly and briefly illustrates the general notion.

and probably most important, there is the Vietnam war. The war has eaten away our image as a nation devoted to international humanitarianism and the defense of freedom and democracy. This erosion has occurred to some degree in all but the most chauvinistic portions of our population. Second, the war conflicted with the antimilitaristic values and ideologies held by many university students. Third, it directly impinged upon the concrete self-interests of many students. Some had their educational careers interrupted by the draft while others were forced to extend their education in order to avoid the draft. For even more the draft introduced uncertainty about their immediate future. Furthermore, it reduced the funds that were available for student aid and improvement of the educational process. In short, the war provided a highly visible and obviously important issue for the society in general and students in particular. It transformed students into one of the major conflict groups in contemporary American society.[16]

Women's Liberation

I have spent a number of pages suggesting how the expansion of education—as one aspect of status inflation—has contributed to the formation and activation of the chosen as one of the major conflict groups in contemporary American society. Now we need to focus on the other major conflict group, the excluded, and attempt to show how the activation of this group is related to status inflation. Actually, the excluded are a set of conflict groups, and each one is a distinctive subculture. As noted earlier, what they share in common is being discriminated against on the basis of some ascribed characteristic. Within the broad category of the excluded are two main subcategories, women and minorities. First, we will deal with the women's liberation movement and then with blacks as a representative of minority conflict groups.

[16] Foreign wars, especially unsuccessful ones, have on several occasions been responsible for crystalizing discontent and opposition within a society. Russia's defeat by Japan in 1905 and unsuccessful participation in World War I is the most obvious example.

The transformation of the excluded into active conflict groups is more readily explained than the radicalization of the chosen. Consequently, they can be treated in considerably less detail.

In the past forty years, there has been a growing tendency for the mass media to portray women as sex objects whose primary purpose is the gratification of men. That men might hold such a view of women is not new. However, the extent that such a view has come to be expressed so explicitly, publicly, and frequently is new. The sources of this phenomenon are complex, but the process of status inflation has contributed in several ways. In Part I, I discussed the tendency for consumer goods to be used as status symbols and to be affected by the process of status inflation. Advertising has obviously played a significant role in the process—and some would argue that it is the primary cause. But if advertising has been a key ingredient in the emphasis on and inflation of status symbols, sex has been a core ingredient in much of this advertising. "Move up (status inflation) to this bigger, more luxurious car (status symbol), and you will be able to acquire this woman (both for sexual gratification and as another status symbol)."

Women's liberation is not simply a revolt against sexism but also against the traditional role of woman as housewife and mother. The increasing participation of married women in the work force has undoubtedly contributed to this dissatisfaction with traditional roles. Moreover, the desire of young families to increase their level of income seems to have been a major cause of married women working. This in turn is at least in part due to the pressures on them to "keep up with the Joneses" which is caused by status inflation.

Many women who have had jobs seem to become increasingly dissatisfied with the social expectation that they also meet the full responsibility of being housewives and mothers. Moreover, in order to live up to the image of women projected in the mass media, especially in advertising, they must also be glamourous sirens. Undoubtedly, the strains of being a regular jobholder, a dutiful wife, and an amateur fashion model are considerable.

But probably the most important aspect of status inflation

for women's liberation is the expansion of higher education, the same aspect that was so important to the genesis of the chosen. For women, as for all students, higher education tends to raise questions about traditional ideologies, including those which relegate women to a subordinate status. Of much more significance is the role that higher education plays in giving women the motivation and skills to pursue a professional career. But a very large percentage of those who are trained and motivated toward professional careers become housewives and find that they have no opportunity to express their professional interests or to use their skills. Those who do find some outlet for their professional interest usually discover, in a very existential way, the realities of sex discrimination. Furthermore, if a professionally active woman is married, the dilemma between job and family is accentuated because her professional activity is more than a job.

In sum, higher education tends to increase the role strain which women suffer, brings into question ideologies which might justify their subordinate position, and gives them the skills to organize effective protest movements.

The Black Revolution

High rates of upward movement and ideological equalitarianism have been central to the white experience in America. The other side of this coin has been discrimination and the doctrine of white supremacy, which have been central to the black experience in America. The opportunities that whites have had for upward mobility have, at least in part, been due to the lack of opportunities for blacks.[17]

If status inflation has created frustration for any sector of our society, it has been the blacks. Although their absolute standard of living has increased as the United States developed economically, they have remained on the bottom, a scorned and segregated caste.

Since the mid-1950s, blacks have increasingly protested their inferior status and have become the most powerful anti-establishment conflict group in our society. The emergence of

[17] See Lipset and Bendix, p. 80.

the civil rights movement and its transformation into the more militant black power movement is a complex historical phenomenon.[18] I propose, however, that the expansion of education has played a more important role than is generally recognized.

First, education has had an important effect on the ideology of the white population; the doctrines of white superiority become more and more untenable. I am not suggesting that higher levels of education have removed all or even most of the racism which has been a historic part of America. However, at the very least, education tends to reduce blatant forms of expression and practice. In addition, educated people are probably less prejudiced in their real (as contrasted with measured or expressed) attitudes as well as in their words and actions than uneducated people. Neither am I suggesting that a change in white attitudes has been the primary cause of the improving treatment and opportunities for blacks. It has, however, weakened efforts to retard and repress demands for racial justice. Whites have tended to defend and protect their vested interests. But such defenses are nearly always less adamant and less successful when you doubt the justice of your cause and suspect that justice is on the side of your opponents.

Second, the expansion of schooling has raised the educational attainment of blacks as well as whites. As in the case of students and women, educational attainment has better prepared black leaders to organize successful protest movements. Probably even more important, the masses of the black community have become more accessible to black leaders. Nearly all receive sophisticated information and propaganda through black-oriented mass media—posters, handbills, newsletters, and so on. These forms of communication were much less significant when the majority of the black community were only semiliterate. (At the turn of the century, 45 per cent of nonwhites were classified by the census as illiterate.) Finally, increasing levels of education enable blacks to skillfully attack the hollowness of the white

---

[18] For some details of the earlier stages see K. Clark, "The Civil Rights Movement: Momentum and Organization," *Daedalus*, 1966, *95*, 239–267.

man's value commitments by pointing out: (1) the contradiction between the ideology of equality and the treatment of blacks; and (2) the intellectual absurdities in doctrines of racial superiority.

The third, and probably most important, effect of expanded schooling has been to generate an important tension or contradiction in the social status of blacks. The gap between black and white levels of education has been reduced dramatically whereas the gap in other measures of welfare has changed relatively little. In part II, we saw that between 1950 and 1965, the gap between black and white levels of education steadily decreased but that the gap in incomes remained about the same. (See Table 1.) Long-term information on the relationship between black and white incomes is not available,[19] but other measures of human welfare such as infant mortality rates and life expectancy figures are available, dating back to the early part of the century. Although the absolute level of welfare has increased steadily for both whites and nonwhites, these data show that the relative gap between blacks and whites has remained the same or decreased by only modest amounts. For some measures, the gap between whites and blacks has actually increased. (See Table 2.)

In 1915, the ratio of nonwhite to white infant mortality was 1.8. In 1970, the ratio was 1.8. That is, both now and fifty-five years ago, the nonwhite rate of infant deaths was almost twice as high as the white rate. During that period, the ratio was nearly constant. The smallest gap was in 1920 when the ratio was 1.6, and the biggest gap was in 1960 when the ratio was 1.9.

The figures on life expectancy are more encouraging. In 1900, the number of years nonwhites were expected to live was about 30 per cent less than whites; that is, the ratio was .70—nonwhites live about 70 per cent as long as whites. During the past seventy years, about two-thirds of the gap has been eliminated

[19] The gap was closed somewhat during World War II. In 1939, the only year prior to 1947 for which data are available, the median family income for nonwhites was only about 40 per cent of the white median income, whereas after the war, the figure had risen to about 50 percent.

Table 1

Ratio of Nonwhite to White Median Family Incomes
and Median Years of Schooling

Year	Income Ratio	Schooling Ratio (ages 25–29)
1940	.39 [a]	.66
1947	.51	
1949	.53	
1950	.51	.71
1951	.54	
1952	.53	
1953	.57	
1954	.56	
1955	.55	
1956	.53	
1957	.54	.80
1958	.51	
1959	.52	
1960	.55	.89
1961	.53	
1962	.53	
1963	.56	
1964	.55	
1965	.60	.96
1966	.60	
1967	.62	.97

Source: Income ratios for 1947–67 taken from US Bureau of the Census, *Current Population Reports*, P-60, No. 59, Table 3. Figure for 1940 estimated from *Historical Statistics of the United States*, 1957, Series G, 148–149; education ratios calculated from *ibid*, Series H, 395–406; and *Current Population Reports*, P-20, No. 182, Table 1; US Bureau of the Census, *Statistical Abstract of the United States: 1968*, Table 157; and US Office of Education, *Digest of Educational Statistics: 1969*.

[a] Based on reports of income during 1939.

until the ratio is about .90. This statistic means that nonwhites still have lives which are about 10 per cent shorter than whites; more concretely, they live, on the average, 6.7 years less. Al-

Table 2

The Ratios of Nonwhite to White
Measures of Welfare

Year	Median Years of Schooling (for those ages 25–29)	Infant Mortality Rate	Life Expectancy at Birth
1890	.19		
1900	.41		.70
1910	.49		.71
1915	—	1.8	.73
1920	.60	1.6	.82
1930	.67	1.7	.78
1940	.66	1.7	.83
1950	.71	1.7	.87
1960	.88	1.9	.90
1970	.97	1.8 [a]	.91 [a]

Source: Calculated from *Historical Statistics of the United States*, Series B101–112, and US Bureau of the Census, *Statistical Abstract of the United States: 1970*, Table 69.

[a] Figures for 1968.

though this measure of welfare shows a definite move toward equality, the rate of change has hardly been dramatic, and a significant amount of inequality remains.

The most dramatic changes have been in the rates of maternal mortality—the percentage of women who die in childbirth. The gap between whites and blacks has *increased*. About 1915, the ratio was 1.8; nonwhite women died in childbirth a little less than twice as often as white women. Forty years later, in 1955, the ratio was almost 4.0. In 1970, the ratio had decreased slightly to about 3.5; nonwhite women die about three and one-half times more frequently than white women, and this gap is almost twice as great as it was in 1915.

Before we go any further, let me emphasize again that these figures look at the *relative* position of whites and nonwhites.

The absolute rates have improved dramatically for both whites and blacks. Moreover, we do not know how much these indicators reflect changes in other aspects of welfare, for example, nutrition, housing, economic security, and so on.

Nonetheless, when all of these qualifications are made, the fact still remains that for the measures available the degree of relative deprivation suffered by blacks has changed very little in this century.

As indicated earlier, the one clear exception to this pattern of deprivation is in the realm of education. The gains in this area have been dramatic compared to the other measures. In 1890, nonwhites received only about one fifth as much schooling as whites.[20] By 1910, they received about one-half as much education. In 1920, the ratio was .60 while in 1940, it had reached .66. The rate of catch-up slowed during this period because of the rapid expansion of secondary education. The level of education of whites increased rapidly. Surprisingly, even during this period, the rate of increase was greater for nonwhites than for whites. Since 1940, when nonwhites received about two-thirds as much schooling as whites, the gap has closed at a much faster rate until by 1970, nonwhites were receiving virtually the same number of years of schooling as whites.[21]

Some of the consequences that result simply from higher levels of education have already been discussed. I now want to focus on the significance of the contradiction between the rapid movement toward equality in education and the slow movement toward equality in other areas. I suspect that slowly but surely the contradiction made it clear to blacks that they could not earn equality. No amount of competence would make the blacks "worthy" of equal treatment by a racist system controlled by whites. Although "good niggers" or "smart niggers" might be

[20] Although the accuracy of these early figures is admittedly questionable, it seems unlikely that the ratio for 1890 would be higher than .30, which would mean that nonwhites would have received about one-third as much schooling as whites.

[21] The median years of schooling for those in the twenty-five through twenty-nine age cohort definitely overstates the extent of educational equality, but this overstatement does not change the fact that there has been considerable progress, both relatively and absolutely.

treated marginally better than the members of their race who were less "worthy," they would never be treated as equal human beings deserving of respect and dignity. It seems at least plausible that this realization was a major social process leading to the civil rights movement with its emphasis on confronting the white society with demands for equality and integration.

I am not, of course, suggesting that this process was conscious. Blacks did not explicitly become aware of the contradiction between education and other aspects of welfare. Rather, the increasing awareness was an underlying structural process resulting in those widely shared, semiconscious predispositions to action which are the stuff of social movements.

But widespread frustrations and predispositions to act must be transformed into mass actions. As I suggested earlier, certain critical historical events were probably important to this triggering process. I made the rather unoriginal point that the Vietnam war played this role for student frustration. World War II may have played a different but equally critical role in triggering the centuries of frustration that went into the civil rights movement. As the figures in Table 1 show, there was a definite improvement in the absolute *and the relative* income of nonwhites during World War II. This increase was almost certainly due to the labor shortages during the war years. But after the war was over and the black man's labor was not so urgently needed, progress in closing the gap almost stopped. I find it hard to imagine that such an experience would not greatly intensify the black man's frustration and increase his cynicism toward white society.

If the sources of the civil rights movement are complex, the causes of its transformation to militancy and black power seem almost infinite. Although some of the internal dynamics of the civil rights movement and the black community were clearly important, I want to point out again the even more obvious significance of the Vietnam war. Interestingly, a sequence of events occurred which were similar to those which occurred during and following World War II. Hopes and expectations were raised by the ideological successes of the civil rights movement in the early 1960s, for instance, the March on Washington in September of 1963 and the passage of the Civil Rights Act of that year. But, as the Vietnam war escalated, the resources for the War on Poverty expanded, but were much less than had been anticipated. Furthermore, the effect of the resources that were allocated was less impressive than had been hoped. There simply was not a concrete improvement in the life and welfare of blacks proportionate to the hopes raised. In addition, greatly disproportionate numbers of blacks were (1) drafted, (2) sent into combat, and (3) killed and wounded. The fruits of this experience are likely to remain bitter for years to come.

Blacks are the largest minority that has been subjected to discrimination, but not the only one. Although we cannot be sure that the same processes were operating within other minority groups, they too have evolved vocal protest movements. It is likely that all minorities have been affected by the processes related to status inflation, but this hypothesis must remain tentative.

Conclusions

In Part III, we have focused on how and why the levels of social conflict have varied in twentieth-century America. First, we briefly considered Marx's predictions that capitalist societies would be overcome by the growing alienation of the working class, leading eventually to violent revolution. Next, we considered some of the structural changes in capitalist societies that have supposedly prevented or at least postponed such an outcome. Third, we focused on attempts to explain why the United States has been more politically stable and had lower levels of class conflict than most other Western industrial societies. Finally, we noted how levels of overt social conflict have increased drastically in the past decade and have raised serious questions about the possibility of continued political stability. I suggested that both the long period of stability and the more recent period of conflict could in part be explained by the process of status inflation and more specifically by the expansion of educational opportunities.

This thesis must, of course, be qualified. No single social process can adequately explain events as complex as those we have considered. Most of the propositions that have been suggested must be considered preliminary hypotheses, and the overall interpretation must be treated as tentative. But the primary purpose of this analysis has not been to develop a validated explanation, but rather to suggest that education and schooling should be viewed in a more balanced perspective than has been common in America in the past. My intent has not been to deny all of the values that are normally attributed to education, but to highlight relationships and consequences that are often overlooked. For only if we see both sides of the coin will we best realize the hopes which have led to our preoccupation with schooling.

Now let me summarize the transformation that has occurred as a result of our long period of educational expansion and status inflation. Earlier, we saw that Marx's predictions about the future of capitalism centered on two main points. First, production would become increasingly centralized and more and more people would become wage laborers. Second, this process would necessarily produce greater and greater alienation among the working class leading to severe class conflict and eventual revolution.

The degree of overt alienation which Marx anticipated has simply not materialized in the working class—regardless of whether we define the working class as all wage laborers or restrict it to blue-collar workers. In fact, the blue-collar workers are the most patriotic sector of the American population. Their enthusiasm has provided important ideological support for the present economic and political system and has been primarily responsible for the development of an important new sector of the capitalistic economy: the production of American-flag decals and "Love It or Leave It" bumper stickers.

Consequently, the focal point of social conflict has not been between workers and those who control the means of production. The primary cleavage has not even been between those who have wealth and those who live off their currently earned income. Therefore, the major social cleavages and conflicts of recent years have not been class conflicts, either in strict Marxian terminology or in more general concepts of social class. For, as we saw when we discussed the concepts of social class, status groups, and political parties (as elaborated by Max Weber), so-cial class focuses on differences in economic position—and this has not been the axis of social conflict. What we have had in re-cent years is greater and greater social strife because of the increasing alienation of certain status groups which I have la-belled the excluded and the chosen. The alienation of these two status groups has in large measure been due to the general process of status inflation and particularly to the expansion of education.

In sum, the class conflict predicted by Marx has first been muted and then transformed into status-group conflict largely by the process of status inflation and especially by the expansion of education. But economic or class factors have become irrelevant. To the contrary the basic prerequisites for status inflation are significant economic inequality and an emphasis on equality of opportunity. Rather than discounting the importance of eco-nomic factors, I want to stress their importance. But I have tried to avoid the mistake of attributing our social divisions and con-flicts to simple differences in economic position. Status-group conflict cannot be reduced to class conflict. The link is there, but it is indirect and complex. Now let us turn directly to the matter of economic inequality and some of its implications for social policy and social theory.

Implications

Nine

The American preoccupation with education has in large measure been aimed at making democracy work and mitigating the tensions created by economic and social differences. A major purpose of this book has been to question the common assumption that we can solve many of our social problems by raising the educational level of underprivileged groups. But education is not the only realm where we seek goals that are made elusive by status inflation.

The War on Poverty was conceived largely as a means of raising the standard of living of those on the bottom. For the most part, issues of inequality and vested interest were avoided. When such issues began to be raised by ghetto community leaders and antipoverty field workers, congressional and local political reaction transformed the assault on poverty into a holding action and in some cases into a full-scale retreat.

139

Health is another area where we have tried to prop up an inherently unequal and ineffective system by piecemeal programs for the poor and the old. Experts almost universally agree that such programs as Medicare and Medicaid have not only failed to provide the underprivileged with adequate medical care, but they have, in many ways, exacerbated the weakness of the present health-care system. In New York City, an attempt was made to provide the poor with quality health care by affiliating each city hospital with a major medical school. This system was supposed to make expert professional staff members, who could provide the knowledge and supervision required for up-to-date, humane health care, available to the hospitals. Affiliations between medical schools and hospitals for the underprivileged have been tried in many cities. The results have been almost universally disappointing and in some cases considerably worse. Miriam Ostow, after a careful study of the New York City affiliation program, concludes:

> The affiliation experience has been, in a sense, analogous to the Medicare-Medicaid experience: the extension of additional resources to the poor and to the institutions serving the poor has not equalized the services available in a complex, unequal system. Perhaps the lesson of these large-scale reform efforts should be the bold and unequivocal recognition that a dual system precludes equality. In that case, policy and program formulation must be directed at rationalization of function and structure in the two systems in order to optimize a defined output rather than to pursue an illusory, if time-honored, objective.[1]

Urban growth and expansion is another area where status inflation has brought not only frustration, but near disaster. The recent history of our urban areas has in large measure been the history of multistepped migration out of the center city. As with education, the well-to-do have struggled to stay a step ahead of the poor. First, they moved to suburbs relatively close to the

[1] M. Ostow, "Affiliation Contracts," in *Urban Health Services, The Case Of New York*, 1970, p. 118.

city. As urban decay—meaning lower-class migration—spread, they moved farther out. In some cities, this process has repeated itself over and over. As an article in *The New York Times* said: "The people of the Outer City are disturbed . . . that they are running out of places to move to. Many have moved from a farm or another country to the central city, then to a close-in suburb, then to a farther-out suburb, and they are tired of moving." [2]

At the core of the problem is the issue of inequality, the unwillingness of the haves to shares with—or more accurately live with—the have nots. To quote *The New York Times* again: "Yet a common trait stands out in virtually all of them [the Outer City and suburban communities]: a turning inward, a determination to shut out the decay and social upheavals of the central city, a lack of concern about the spreading agony and distress only a few miles away . . . Interviews with scores of community leaders showed the protectiveness and insularity to be surprisingly pervasive and widespread. Here are some of the signs: . . ." The articles goes on to describe the situation in six outer cities in Ohio, Maryland, California, and Georgia.

More than in other types of status inflation, race is a critical factor behind the movement from bad neighborhoods to good neighborhoods, from inner cities to outer cities. Whites flee the inner city which is taken over by blacks. But the problem is not only—and possibly not primarily—racism. The same cycle of moving farther and farther out occurs in the black communities.

"We are an inner-city suburb with all the problems of the central city," remarked Mr. Chandler, the articulate, East Cleveland city manager. He said that larger and poorer families were moving in, taxing the city's services and schools and reducing its revenue and thereby causing fast deterioration. A few blacks

---

[2] John Herbers, "The Outer City: Uneasiness over the Future," *The New York Times*, June 2, 1971. This article is part of a five-article series on the problems of suburban outer cities, appearing in *The New York Times* between May 30, and June 3, 1971. I cite and quote this series not because it is a definitive scholarly source, but because it illustrates that the process and problems I am alluding to are well known and widely discussed.

*whose incomes grow move on to other outer cities, such as
Shaker Heights and Cleveland Heights, he said.*

*The same complaint was registered by the Compton, California,
city manager, James Johnson, thirty-seven years old, quiet, and
like Mr. Chandler, black. Mr. Johnson said that Compton was
a town of middle-class Negro professionals—blacks are 70 per
cent of the city's 78,611 residents—but they were moving farther
out in the outer city, most to bordering Carson, leaving as
replacements low-income families with more children and more
problems.*[3]

The article goes on to note that the head of Citizens for
Open Housing in the Cleveland, Ohio, area "believes that race
is disappearing as a factor and that people are at least willing
to accept well-to-do Negroes into their neighborhoods. 'The
big question then is about the poor,' she said. 'There is not a
political force for them.'" These comments probably under-
estimate the degree to which racism is still the key factor.
Nonetheless, even if the problem of racism were eliminated,
economic inequality would continue to produce the migration-
decay-migration syndrome.

Economic Equality: The Undiscussed Issue

The failure of the War on Poverty, the crisis in health
care, and urban-suburban decay, as well as many other of our
current social problems, are inextricably intertwined with the
process of status inflation and our failure to deal with the issue
of economic inequality. The standard liberal assumption has been
that we can do much more for those on the bottom and everyone else if we concentrate on expanding the size of the pie
rather than on how it should be divided. Since World War II,
it has been considered boorish to be too insistent about issues
of economic inequality. To raise such issues was bad taste and
bad tactics which could create resistance to needed reform and
social welfare programs. To demand that the issue of economic

[3] P. Delaney, "The Outer City: Negroes Find Few Tangible
Gains," *The New York Times*, June 1, 1971.

inequality be faced explicitly and made part of the national debate was considered naive and utopian. The public considered it an illusion to think that our national life could be improved by explicitly considering and dealing with the issue of economic inequality. The only realistic hope, so the standard liberal theory went, was to improve the lot of the underprivileged gradually as the total wealth of the nation expanded.

There are times, however, when the only realistic policy for the long run is an unrealistic stance for the short run. This is the case, I think, with the issue of inequality. But, of course, the question is not inequality in abstract, but how much inequality. In 1968, the top 10 per cent of the families received 30 per cent of the national income, whereas the bottom 10 per cent received 1 per cent of the national income. That is, the top 10 per cent made, on the average, *thirty times* as much as the bottom 10 per cent. There are good up-to-date figures on the distribution of accumulated wealth (contrasted with the income earned during a given year). It seems unlikely that lack of interest or the protestations of the poor are responsible for this void in our knowledge. At any rate, the distribution of accumulated wealth is almost certainly even more unequal because high-income groups save a greater proportion of their income than do low-income groups.

My own inclinations are to be suspicious of utopian notions of complete economic equality. But surely the current degree of economic inequality can be reduced several times over before we have to deal with the problems of a full-fledged utopia.

How can we bring about reductions in economic inequality? A minimum and maximum on income and wealth might be one way to start the process. But proposals, solutions, and answers will have to await another time and another place. My purpose in this book is not to resolve the issue but to stimulate the debate. Highlighting the possibilities and consequences will be one of the critical functions of such a debate.

I am not unaware that the topic has been discussed before during the history of mankind, and I have no illusions that there is a final solution. But there are proximate solutions which offer the possibilities for a significantly better society and world than we have today. I have little hope for such a world unless the issue is faced and we develop a solution that is more just and humane than we have known before.

The Future of Educational Opportunity

Those who have persevered and read this far are indubitably aware that I have misgivings about our national preoccupation with educational opportunity. Although we have vastly expanded the facilities for education and the amount of schooling that people receive, this has had little effect on equality of educational opportunity for different social classes. Children from high-SES families have continued to receive significantly more and better schooling than children from low-SES families. Moreover, the degree of inequality and inequality of opportunity with respect to jobs, income, and wealth have remained largely unchanged. Consequently, I have suggested that if we want to reduce inequalities with respect to the distribution of and the life chances for jobs, income, and wealth, we should attack this issue directly. That is, our efforts must be aimed directly at a redistribution of wealth and income—by new tax laws, for example—rather than at equality of opportunity for education. We have too long labored under the illusion that the structures of inequality can be significantly changed by dabbling with the education system.

But to argue that we must concentrate directly on the distribution of income and wealth does not mean that I am unconcerned about inequality of opportunity in education. Nor do I think that success in reducing economic inequality will automatically reduce unequal opportunities for schooling. Consequently, some comments are in order about the future relationship of economic inequality and inequality of opportunity for education.

But equalizing the resources available to pay for education is a less important effect of greater economic equality than is the potential effect on values and life styles. The well-to-do have values and attitudes which encourage academic performance and achievement, whereas these attitudes are less developed in

the lower classes. In Part II, I presented evidence to indicate
that the primary bottleneck to education was lack of motivation
rather than lack of money. It may seem paradoxical then to
argue that the way to equalize motivation is to equalize economic resources. But there is a critical difference between
changing a family's basic economic position in society and
simply providing it with additional money to meet the cost
of higher education. Values and attitudes are shaped by the
economic milieu to which people belong. Several years ago,
Herbert Hyman summarized many of the available findings
on the relationship between economic position and values.[4] For
example, Hyman found that the children of the "wealthy and
prosperous" consistently had a stronger preference for college
than did the children of individuals from lower-socioeconomic
backgrounds. For males fourteen to twenty years old, 74 per
cent of the wealthy or prosperous recommended a college
education compared with 63 per cent of the middle class and
42 per cent of the lower class. The class differences were even
larger for females. Greater class differences were also observed
in the parents' recommendations concerning college. Similar
class differences were found with respect to occupations desired,
work values, and perceptions of opportunities. There is also a
well known relationship between social class and child-rearing
patterns. This is, of course, a key link between the social class
of parents and the values and attitudes of their children.[5]

If economic position influences values, attitudes, and socialization patterns (which in turn influence educational opportunities), how quickly do changes in the economic structure
influence these other social and cultural factors? Possibly we
can gain some clues from commonplace observations about the
nouveau riche. Individuals who acquire new wealth often make
drastic changes in their living patterns but frequently are unable
to acquire the more subtle behaviors and attitudes required for

[4] H. H. Hyman, "The Value Systems of Different Classes." See
also H. Hodges, *Social Stratification*, Chapters 7–11.
[5] See U. Bronfenbrenner, "Socialization and Social Class Through
Time and Space," and Hodges, Chapter 9.

full social acceptance by the traditionally wealthy. But if the new wealth is maintained, there is a great probability that the behavior and attitudinal patterns of the children will be generally indistinguishable from the patterns of children whose families have a long history of wealth. Certainly, this has happened by the grandchildrens' generation. If these impressionistic observations are accurate, and if the nouveau riche are an appropriate model for how changes in economic position affect values and attitudes, then we could expect an equalization of the economic structure to have significant effects on first-generation children and some additional effects on the second generation.

The nouveau riche model may actually overstate the time required because the upper class is probably more rigorous in its selectivity and screening procedures than are other subgroups and may continue to discriminate against those with new wealth even when the latter conform to upper-class norms. Consequently, a redistribution of income and wealth may affect values and attitudes, especially motivation for education, more rapidly than the nouveau riche model indicates. But this model has other limitations which may flaw its predictive power in more crucial ways. First, it focuses on extreme change in economic condition and change only in one direction—up. Second, it considers the relationship between changes in economic level and changes in values, attitudes, and general behavior rather than dealing specifically with the effect of economic position on educational opportunity.

We have, however, some quantitative research which focuses specifically on the relationship between family economic position and the educational progress of the children. Both John Conlisk and Stanley Masters have studied the factors which influence attendance and performance in elementary and secondary school. Conlisk concludes that most factors related to performance and attendance are outside the control of either the children or the policy makers. "The major exception to this would seem to be parental income. . . . The [statistical analysis] predicts that the increase in parent's income will result in significant increases in their children's school enrollment and performance. This suggests a mechanism by which income supplements to poor parents may have desirable second-generation effects on poverty." [6] Masters, in a parallel study, comes to a similar, though slightly more pessimistic, conclusion. "While the short-run effects are likely to be quite small, the long-run effects may be especially important." [7]

The nouveau-riche model and this quantitative research suggest that we may have been trying to put the cart before the horse. For years, we have been expanding educational facilities and opportunities in order to bring the performance level of lower socioeconomic group individuals up so they can earn adequate rewards. But one of the central arguments of this book is that we should at least seriously consider approaching the problem from the opposite direction. It took us many years to learn that economic depressions require government spending, not economy. We may be in a similar process of learning that economic equality must precede rather than follow meaningful educational equality of opportunity.

Although the nouveau-riche model and the research by Conlisk and Masters are suggestive, they do not deal directly with the question of whether greater economic equality will produce more equal educational opportunities. The research and the model focus on changes in individual (and family) position within a given structure rather than changes of the structure itself. Needed historical comparisons of cases with a significant reduction in inequality within a generation or two would enable us to correlate reductions in inequality with change in values and change in educational opportunities. Instances of rapid economic equalization are extremely rare, and instances where data are available are even more rare. However, three cases come to mind which may at least hint at the probable

[6] J. Conlisk, "Determinants of School Enrollment and School Performance," *The Journal of Human Resources*, 1969, *4*, 157.

[7] S. H. Masters, "The Effect of Family Income on Children's Education: Some Findings on Inequality of Opportunity," *The Journal of Human Resources*, 1969, *4*, 159. To some extent, the focus of this article is race inequality rather than class inequality, but the article's findings have definite implications for how changes in the income structure might reduce both types of inequality.

relationship between economic inequality and educational opportunity.

The first is the United States. As we have seen, attempts
to increase educational opportunity and economic equality
through the expansion of schooling have been largely ineffectual.

The second case is Sweden where to some extent the
opposite process has been under way. For over a generation,
Sweden has had an explicit policy of reducing income differences. This policy has been carried out primarily by granting
larger wage increases to the lower classes than to the middle
and professional class. However, compared with the United
States, Sweden has maintained a relatively elitist higher-
educational system. For example, when Joseph Ben-David carried out a comparative study of the professions and higher
education in the early 1960s, Sweden had 6.36 college graduates
per 10,000 population compared with 25.06 for the United
States. Although Sweden has probably the highest standard of
living after the United States, fifteen nations, including the
Philippines, Iceland, and India, had a higher ratio of college
graduates.[8] In early 1971, Sweden had a series of labor strikes
and lockouts by professionals—including college professors and
army officers—protesting the failure of the government to grant
them wage increases comparable to those granted working-class
groups.

Undoubtedly, many factors contributed to the Swedish
situation, but the failure to expand opportunities for higher
education at a rate more comparable with that in other highly
developed nations may very well play an important role in
the recent resistance to further equalization of income. Sweden
has a gradation of income differences rather than distinct classes,
and the distance between those on the bottom and those on the
top has been steadily reduced. This relative inequality and inequality of opportunity in education may handicap further re-

[8] J. Ben-David, "The Growth of the Professions and the Class
System," *Current Sociology*, 1963–1964, *12*, 256–257. The data he uses
are for 1958. There has been no significant change in relative position in
more recent years.

ductions in economic inequality because those who consider themselves qualitatively superior with respect to training resent attempts to further eliminate differences in income.

The third case which comes to mind is Russia. A decrease in economic inequality and a concerted attempt to expand opportunities for education occurred after the revolution in 1917. In 1931, Stalin made a famous speech against "equality-mongering." For almost twenty-five years following his speech, there was an intensification of economic inequality. At the same time, opportunities for higher education became more restricted, and the children of the elite had a definite advantage. After Khrushchev gained power, Russia experienced another reversal, and it seems that both economic rewards and educational opportunities have become significantly more equal.[9]

What these three cases suggest—each in a different way— is that there are probably fairly narrow limits within which it is possible to increase either economic equality or educational opportunity independently. This realization brings us almost full circle. The main argument of this book has been that further expansion of educational opportunities will not significantly reduce inequality or inequality of opportunity. The main argument of this section has been that greater economic equality will probably increase equality of opportunity in the educational sphere. Now I want to argue that if we want to make a serious attempt to eliminate inequality of educational opportunity we are going to have to reduce *both* economic inequality *and* develop special programs aimed specifically at equalizing opportunities for education.

Earlier, we argued that greater economic equality would contribute to greater educational equality of opportunity. But the possibilities should not be overstated. In 1971, the address

[9] For discussions of economic and educational inequality in the Soviet Union, see A. Inkeles, "Social Stratification and Mobility in the Soviet Union: 1940–1950," *American Sociological Review*, 1950, *15*, 465–479; R. A. Feldmesser, "Equality and Inequality Under Khrushchev," *Problems of Communism*, 1960, *9*, 31–39; and M. Yanowitch, "The Soviet Income Revolution," *Slavic Review*, 1963, *22*, 683–697. The first two are reprinted in R. Bendix and S. Lipset, *Class, Status, and Power*. The third is reprinted in Heller, *Structured Social Inequality*.

given at the American Sociological Association's national meetings by its president, William Sewell, focused on inequality of opportunity for higher education. He comments specifically on the limitations of programs intended to affect family incomes:

One would have wished that family income might have had a larger and a more special set of effects on opportunities for higher education because it is the aspect of background most readily amenable to change. But our evidence raises doubt that the programs based on family-income supplementation alone will result in any rapid and marked reduction in inequality in higher education. This is not to deny the importance of income . . . but it is to warn that family-income programs, however desirable they may be for reducing other social inequalities, will not bring about quick or dramatic results in overcoming inequality of higher education. Certainly, we should not rely on this means alone to bring about equalization of opportunities for higher education.[10]

Sewell goes on to argue for a "more targeted" approach based on grants to students strictly according to need, maintenance of low tuition, and programs of compensatory education for children from disadvantaged backgrounds.

Sewell's warning must be taken seriously. However, a systematic reduction in economic inequalities is a considerably more basic change than is supplementing the family-income of the poor—which is the alternative toward which his remarks are directed. Consequently, the effects of such a reduction in economic inequality of opportunities for education may be considerably greater than Sewell's remarks seem to suggest. In my opinion, his proposals again put the cart before the horse. But it would be foolish if, after turning the horse and cart around and getting them in proper sequence, we led the horse away without having hitched up the cart.

A postscript is appropriate about a new development

[10] W. H. Sewell, "Inequality of Opportunity for Higher Education," *American Sociological Review*, 1971, *36*, 801.

concerning equality of educational opportunity. My analysis of the relationship between education and inequality has concentrated on higher education because elementary and secondary education are already in some senses universal. During the last half of the 1960s, debates over educational opportunity centered on opportunities for a college education. But as the lower class and minority groups began to press for opportunities to go to college, they encountered what for them was a new problem. In the eyes of God and the traditional job market, all high school graduates may have educational credentials that are roughly equal. However, in the eyes of college admission offices, some are more equal than others.[11] This, along with other developments, has focused new attention on differences in the quality of pre-college education.

In 1971, there were important court rulings in California, Minnesota, and Texas that declared existing methods of financing public education unconstitutional. The basis of these decisions was that schools were financed by property taxes which meant that the tax base available to different communities varied drastically depending on local property values. The result was that the per pupil expenditure in well-to-do communities was sometimes more than double the expenditure in poor communities. We apparently are moving toward court decisions that will require per pupil expenditures for elementary and secondary education to be roughly the same within a given state. Possibly this equalization of resources could be extended to public colleges. Admittedly, this would be a significant departure from the past. Will equalizing expenditure per pupil in public schools truly equalize educational opportunities? I think not. More precisely I suspect that it will further reduce racial inequalities but have little effect on class inequalities. For despite statements and rhetoric to the contrary, it is quite likely that not only will poor school districts be given more resources per pupil, wealthy school districts will be forced to reduce per

[11] While special quotas for minority students have lessened difficulties and frustrations for the time being, they have not and cannot solve the basic problem.

pupil expenditure. To avoid such a reduction would require tax increases that lower-income groups cannot pay and that upper-income groups will not tolerate—at least when there is another strategy open to them. That strategy is to fight for low tax rates—and put their own children in private schools.

This is not to say that such an outcome is inevitable. But given our past experience in these matters skepticism is called for. Instead of becoming an effective means of equalizing educational opportunity, the equalization of per pupil expenditure could easily become the new liberal illusion, and the next stage of status inflation in the educational system.

Expansion of Rights

In the last section, we focused on the relationship between two different dimensions of inequality: education and economic resources (i.e., money and property). There are of course many different dimensions of inequality. A very important part of the history of the modern world is how greater equality was achieved first along one or two of these many dimensions and then extended to another dimension.

T. H. Marshall argues that the modern trend toward equality can in large measure be understood as the expansion of the basic rights men were due by virtue of their citizenship in the nation-state. Whether or not an individual is a full member or participant in a nation-state is dependent upon his citizenship status. Supposedly everyone who holds the status of citizen is entitled, simply by virtue of his citizenship, to certain basic rights. Since the eighteenth century, there has tended to be a gradual but steady expansion of these rights. According to Marshall, the first stage in the modern trend toward equality was the attainment of civil rights: freedom of speech, religion, the right to own property or to enter any occupation, equal treatment before the law, and so on. We often forget that only a few hundred years ago these rights were not available or that some groups were given special privileges while others were denied virtually all of these rights by custom, law, or both. Next came the development of political rights, primarily the right of ordinary citizens to vote and hold office. Steadily, barriers such as property requirements, race, and sex have been eliminated, at least in principle. The most recent extention of these rights in the United States has been the inclusion of young adults by lowering the voting age to eighteen. The third dimension was social rights: certain basic levels of social welfare. These rights are expressed in benefits such as publicly financed old-age pensions, unemployment insurance, health insurance, and, maybe most of all, education.[12]

Marshall's insightful observations become more meaningful if we look for the relationship between each step or stage. To at least some degree, the demand for equality in new areas can be seen as an attempt to actualize equalities that have in principle already been won. For example, people quickly discovered that civil rights which were granted by law were often very hard to obtain from political officials who were largely removed from effective public pressure. At least in part, the push for political democracy was a demand for a governmental structure that would provide in practice the civil rights already granted in theory. The extension of social rights, especially public education, was specifically seen as a means for citizens to realize in fact the political rights that were supposedly theirs. In Part I, we noted that since the very early period of our republic, the expansion of education was advocated as a necessary prerequisite for meaningful political democracy.

Certainly, the expansion of basic rights to more and more sectors of collective life has brought greater levels of real equality. Yet one does not need to be very radical to recognize that the extent to which an individual is able to realize his rights in all of these areas is much affected by his economic position. It is one thing to have the right to hire a good lawyer and quite another thing to have the money to do so. All have the right to become a presidential candidate; only a minuscule portion—even of the highly talented white gentiles—have the economic resources necessary to do so.

We have by no means been oblivious to this difficulty, but a solution has not been easy. We confront again the basic

[12] T. H. Marshall, *Citizenship and Social Class.*

dilemma that was discussed in Part I: the contradiction between our value on equality and our value on achievement. All should be equal with regard to certain basic rights, but economic position should for the most part be determined by one's own achievements. As indicated earlier, our basic response to this dilemma has been to help all to acquire the tools needed to earn a comfortable and secure economic position. We have seen education as the means to this end.

To even the most optimistic, it has been clear that we have not fully succeeded in this endeavor. To even the most enthusiastic advocate, it has been apparent that this means has limits, not only in practice but in principle. The sick, the old, and the young simply cannot earn their own way no matter what kind of education, training, or tools they are given. In addition, many are unemployed from time to time—even though they have skills and talents—because of fluctuations in the economy. For others, the problem is more serious. The skills which they have spent years acquiring become obsolete long before they are ready to retire from the work force, yet late enough in their careers so that retraining is at best difficult and expensive.

The unemployed and unemployable bring us to a second reason for our expansion of social rights. Our first response has been to help people earn their way—primarily through more education. Our second response has been to attempt to provide a basic minimum of social services to all—whether they earn it or not. Steadily, if reluctantly, we have assigned the government the responsibility for providing this basic level of welfare to those who are unable to make it on their own. Such social services as old age pensions, unemployment insurance, city and county hospitals, medical care for the aged and the poor, aid to dependent children, and "welfare" have been created to provide this basic level of services.

Undoubtedly, these welfare measures have been beneficial for many and have softened some of the worst results of poverty and economic inequality. But these measures have also tended to create two separate sectors in many areas of our social life: those who work for a living and those on welfare.

We have a medical care system for the poor based on outpatient clinics and city hospitals, and medical care for the middle and upper classes based on private physicians and voluntary hospitals. Increasingly, in our urban areas, we have a public school system for the black and the poor and private schools for the middle and upper classes. In many cities, the same divisions seem to be developing between public housing and private housing.

In nearly all of these areas, the well-to-do are able to maintain their privileges by investing their own resources and creating private systems. Not infrequently, these private systems are aided by government subsidies. These private sectors are almost without exception able to attract the most talented and best trained personnel and to secure more modern and up-to-date facilities than similar public services. What seems to occur here is not status inflation at the individual level, but a form of status inflation which affects vast systems of public and private services.

Again and again, our society has defined the problem in terms of lack of resources. I have tried to demonstrate that the primary problem is not a lack of resources, but economic inequality. We are unlikely to make much additional progress in equalizing—in practice, not just in principle—civil, political, or social rights until we face squarely the underlying issue of economic inequality.

Clearly, there are not hard and fast lines either between the various dimensions of inequality or between the various stages in the struggle for greater equality. Neither is it necessary to argue that the stages had to occur in the sequence suggested—although theoretical reasons make this order more likely than some other. I do not mean to suggest that other stages are inevitable or that man progresses relentlessly toward greater equality. But the modern historical experience with equality, particularly in the Western world, has tended to involve these stages which focused on various issues or dimensions of inequality.

I suggest that we need to shift the struggle to another more basic dimension and to a new set of issues. That is, we have reached a point in our history when we need to face directly and explicitly the issue of economic inequality. Our preoccupation with equality of opportunity and particularly with opportunities for education have obscured this need.

Substructures and Revolutions

From a Marxist point of view, this book has dealt with surface matters rather than the root of the problem, with superstructures rather than substructures. For, according to Marx, economic inequality is a result of certain key aspects of a capitalist society—namely the existence of private property or, more precisely, the private ownership of the means of production. Consequently, to talk about reducing economic inequality without discussing the nature and function of private property and the resulting distribution of power is at best naive and probably deliberately obscurantist.

In a certain sense, I plead guilty to not dealing with "substructures," and I recognize this serious limitation. If we place limits on the amounts of income and wealth that private individuals can receive and hold, the question is necessarily raised as to who is to have formal ownership and who is to have effective control of the vast amounts of property that make up our modern industrial system. Greater equality does have implications for the social organization and control of a society's property. The critical question, however, is what are the implications? The traditional Marxist answer was that the means of production should be owned, controlled, and operated by the state. Less traditional Marxists talk of "industrial democracy" and "workers' control." But the records of these schemes have not been particularly promising up to the present. I am not saying that more just, humane systems of distributing and controlling property are impossible. An important task in the years ahead, especially for intellectuals, will be to devise such schemes. But our past innovation and imaginativeness in this area have been meager at best.

But to acknowledge that the focus has been on superstructures is not to admit that we have focused on superficialities. There are two important reasons for analyzing so-called superstructures in some detail. First, such a discussion is a necessary prerequisite for both seeing and dealing with substructures. The second reason is that the problems of superstructures, namely, economic inequality, cannot be simply reduced to a problem of substructure, namely, ownership or control of the industrial system. Let us take as an example the issue that we dealt with in Part III, conflict groups. The Marxian analysis predicts that social conflict will increase and become synonymous with class conflict, conflict between those who own the means of production in industrial society and those who work for wages. Up to now, this conflict has not occurred. In the past decade, the United States has been shaken by some of the most extensive and violent social conflicts of this century. I have argued that these conflicts were primarily between status groups and not social classes. But at the same time, I have tried to show that both the formation and the activation of these conflict groups have been very much related to economic inequality and our attempts to cope with this latter problem by the expansion of educational opportunities. These conflicts are in turn indirectly related to the question of who owns and controls the means of production, but they can not be reduced to that issue.

It is hardly news that social life is complex. Marx was the master of seeing complex interrelationships. But in at least one respect, he thought that the ability to grasp complexities would become less and less essential. As we have noted, he thought that the course of history would simplify our analytical problem. Capitalist society, according to Marx, will become increasingly simplified and polarized between capitalists and workers. The increase in class consciousness will be caused primarily by the social situation which will become more and more obvious, not primarily by the members of the proletariat becoming sophisticated social scientists.[13]

But the opposite may have occurred. The social and

[13] I do not want to overstate this issue. Certainly, Marx gave an important role to intellectual understanding and the development of revolutionary analysis and ideology. Nonetheless, as with most of his analysis, clear priority was given to structural rather than ideological changes.

economic structure of advanced industrial societies has hardly become more simplified. Yet there are signs that society is gaining a greater social consciousness of its problems, limitations, and contradictions. This new way in which people perceive the world is in part due to new levels of knowledge acquired through higher levels of education, that is to ideational changes. For example, higher levels of education have made untenable some of the ideologies which supported old inequities and injustices, for instance, the myth of racial superiority. But education has not only affected what people think; it has also affected what they want. Although the evidence is far from definitive, it seems as if the group that I have called the chosen do have more egalitarian values and are less preoccupied with material wants. These attitudes are probably the result of both affluence and education. But the change in wants and desires is not due simply to intellectual enlightenment. The lengthening and bureaucratization of the schooling process have shown them at an early age and in a very personal way how alienating the rat race and endless striving tends to be. In addition, the hollowness of their parents' life style, with all its affluence, has convinced them that the eventual "rewards" are simply not worth the cost. Consequently, they seem to be defining their self-interest differently from the way previous generations did.

Modern history has not simplified the problem of social consciousness by simplifying the structure of the modern world. Yet possibly we now have a better chance of grasping the reality of our situation because to some degree both our ideas and our interests have been transformed in ways that we did not intend. This new social consciousness should not be identified with progress or enlightenment. To see the world in a clearer light is not by itself to change the world into a better place.

How is this change to come about? The traditional Marxian answer is quite clear. We must go to the heart of the matter and transform the system of property and power relations. Anything less is superficial. But the question which confronts the nontraditional radical of today is whether better alternative systems of property and power relations are available to us now which are worth the cost of implementing. At this point in our history, part of that cost would quite likely be a violent revolution. In addition to the death and destruction that such a revolution would involve, all revolutions create possibilities for regression as well as progress. We might easily loose the civil and political liberties we now have—in however attenuated form—in the process of instituting a more equitable economic order via revolution.

Some unhesitatingly support a revolution. In their eyes the present situation is so evil that almost any conceivable cost or risk is justified. Moreover, they argue that no privileged group will allow a redistribution of income and wealth unless they are literally forced to do so and that to think otherwise is to ignore hard realities and to seek after another impossible illusion. I must confess that history puts much of the evidence on the side of this radical thesis. But not all historical evidence is on that side. Although I cannot say that I am confident about the future, I am still hopeful that basic changes can come about without a major conflagration—though such changes will not occur without conflict and violence. We must face the hard realities, but not become captured by them. For history has a strange way of dealing with hard realities. Not infrequently, yesterday's hard reality becomes the obscuring illusion of today, and today's impossible illusion becomes the necessity for tomorrow. Let us hope that it is so. Let us act to see that it is so.

References

American Council on Education. *The Black Student in American Colleges.* ACE Research Report, 1969, *4* (2).

American Council on Education. *National Norms for College Freshmen—Fall, 1969.* ACE Research Report, 1969, *4* (7).

ASTIN, A. "Undergraduate Achievement and Institutional Excellence." *Science,* Aug. 16, 1968.

BELL, D. *The Radical Right.* Garden City, New York: Doubleday, 1963.

BEN-DAVID, J. "The Growth of the Professions and the Class System." *Current Sociology,* 1963–1964, *12,* 256–277.

BENDIX, R., and LIPSET, S. M. (Eds.) *Class, Status, and Power, Social Stratification in Comparative Perspective* (2nd ed.) New York: Macmillan, 1966.

BERDIE, R. *Decisions for Tomorrow: Plans of High School Seniors.* Minneapolis: University of Minnesota Press, 1965.

BERGER, B. "The New Stage of American Man—Almost Endless Adolescence." *New York Times Magazine,* Nov. 2, 1969.

BIRNBAUM, R., and GOLDMAN, J. *The Graduates: A Follow-Up Study of New York City High School Graduates of 1970.* New York: Center for Social Research and Office for Research in Higher Education, City University of New York, 1971.

BLAU, P., and DUNCAN, O. D. *The American Occupational Structure.* New York: Wiley, 1967.

BOTTOMORE, T. B. Review of P. Blau, and O. D. Duncan, *The American Occupational Structure. American Sociological Review,* 1968, *33,* 295–296.

BRONFENBRENNER, U. "Socialization and Social Class Through Time and Space." In Macoby, E. E., Newcomb, T. M., and Hartley, E. L. (Eds.), *Readings in Social Psychology.* New York: Holt, Rinehart, and Winston, 1958.

Carnegie Commission on Higher Education. *Quality and Equality: New Levels of Federal Responsibility for Higher Education.* New York: McGraw-Hill, 1968.

CLARK, B. *Educating the Expert Society.* San Francisco: Chandler, 1962.

CLARK, H. H. (Ed.) *Thomas Paine, Key Writings.* New York: Hill and Wang, 1961.

CLARK, K. "The Civil Rights Movement: Momentum and Organization." *Daedalus,* 1966, *95,* 239–267.

College Entrance Examination Board. *Report of the Panel on Student Financial Need Analysis.* New York, 1971.

CONLISK, J. "Determinants of School Enrollment and School Performance." *Journal of Human Resources,* 1969, *4,* 140–157.

CRANE, D. "Scientists at Major and Minor Universities." *American Sociological Review,* 1965, *30,* 699–714.

CRANE, D. "Social Class Origin and Academic Success: The Influence of Two Stratification Systems on Academic Careers." *Sociology of Education,* 1969, *42,* 1–17.

CREMIN, L. *The Genius of American Education.* Pittsburgh, Pa.: University of Pittsburgh Press, 1966.

DAHRENDORF, R. *Class and Class Conflict in Industrial Society.* Stanford, Calif.: Stanford University Press, 1959.

DAVIS, J. "The Campus as a Frog Pond: An Application of the Theory of Relative Deprivation to Career Decisions of College Men." *American Journal of Sociology,* 1966, *72,* 17–31.

DAVIS, J. *Career Decisions.* Chicago: Aldine, 1964.

DAVIS, J. *Great Aspirations.* Chicago: Aldine, 1964.

DELANEY, P. "The Outer City: Negroes Find Few Tangible Gains." *The New York Times,* June 1, 1970.

DOMHOFF, G. W. *Who Rules America.* Englewood Cliffs, N.J.: Prentice-Hall, 1967.

DUNCAN, O. D. "Inheritance of Poverty or Inheritance of Race?" In D. P. Moynihan (Ed.), *Understanding Poverty.* New York: Basic Books, 1969.

DUNCAN, O. D. "The Trend of Occupational Mobility in the United States." *American Sociological Review*, 1965, *30*, 491–498.

ECKLAND, B. "Genetics and Sociology: A Reconsideration." *American Sociological Review*, 1967, *30*, 173–194.

ETZIONI, A. *The Active Society*. New York: Macmillan, 1968.

FELDMAN, K., and NEWCOMB, T. *The Impact of College*. San Francisco: Jossey-Bass, 1969. (2 vols.)

FELDMAN, R. A. "Equality and Inequality Under Khrushchev." *Problems of Communism*, 1960, *9*, 31–39.

FLACKS, R. "The Roots of Student Protest." *The Journal of Social Issues*, 1967, *23*, 52–75.

FOLGER, J. K., ASTIN, H. S., and BAYER, A. E. *Human Resources and Higher Education*. New York: Russell Sage Foundation, 1970.

FROOMKIN, J. *Aspirations, Enrollments, and Resources: The Challenge to Higher Education in the Seventies*. Washington, D.C.: Government Printing Office (Office of Education), 1970.

GALBRAITH, J. K. *The Affluent Society*. New York: New American Library, 1958.

GALBRAITH, J. K. *The New Industrial State*. New York: New American Library, 1968.

GUSFIELD, J. R. *Symbolic Crusade*. Urbana, Ill.: University of Illinois Press, 1966.

HANSEN, W. L., and WEISBROD, B. A. *Benefits, Costs, and Finance of Public Higher Education*. Chicago: Markham, 1969.

HARGENS, L. L. "Patterns of Mobility Among New Ph.D's Among American Academic Institutions." *Sociology of Education*, 1969, *42*, 18–37.

HARGENS, L. L., and HAGSTROM, W. O. "Sponsored and Contest Mobility of American Academic Scientists." *Sociology of Education*, 1967, *40*, 24–38.

HELLER, C. S. (Ed.) *Structured Social Inequality: A Reader in Comparative Social Stratification*. New York: Macmillan, 1969.

HERBERS, J. "The Outer City: Uneasiness over the Future." *The New York Times*, June 2, 1971.

HERRIOT, R. A., and MILLER, H. P. "Who Paid the Taxes in 1968?" Unpublished paper read at the National Industrial Conference Board, New York, March 18, 1971.

Historical Statistics of the United States. Washington, D.C.: Government Printing Office, 1957.

HODGES, H. M., JR. *Social Stratification: Class in America*. Cambridge, Mass.: Schenkman, 1964.

HOFSTADTER, R. *The Age of Reform*. New York: Knopf, 1956.

HYMAN, H. H. "The Value Systems of Different Classes." In R. Bendix and S. Lipset (Eds.) *Class, Status, and Power*. (2nd ed.) New York: Macmillan, 1966.

INKELES, A. "Social Stratification and Mobility in the Soviet Union: 1940–1950." *American Sociological Review*, 1950, *15*, 475–479.

JAFFE, A. J., and ADAMS, W. *American Higher Education in Transition*. New York: Bureau of Applied Social Research, Columbia University, 1969.

JENCKS, C., and REISMAN, D. *The Academic Revolution*. Garden City, N.Y.: Doubleday, 1968.

KEMPER, T. D. "Reference Groups, Socialization, and Achievement." *American Sociological Review*, 1965, *33*, 31–45.

KLUCKHOHN, C. *Culture and Behavior*. Glencoe, Ill.: Macmillan, 1962.

KOLKO, G. *Wealth and Power in America*. New York: Praeger, 1962.

LIPSET, S. M. *The First New Nation*. Garden City, N.Y.: Doubleday, 1967.

LIPSET, S. M., and BENDIX, R. *Social Mobility in Industrial Society*. Berkeley and Los Angeles: University of California Press, 1959.

MARSHALL, T. H. *Citizenship and Social Class*. Cambridge, England: University of Cambridge Press, 1950.

MARX, K., and ENGELS, F. *Selected Works in Two Volumes*. Moscow: Foreign Languages Publishing House, 1962.

MASTERS, S. H. "The Effect of Family Income on Children's Education: Some Findings on Inequality of Opportunity." *Journal of Human Resources*, 1969, *4*, 158–175.

METZGER, W. "The Crisis of Academic Authority." *Daedalus*, 1970, *99*, 568–608.

MILLER, H. P. *Income Distribution in the United States*. Washington, D.C.: Government Printing Office, 1966.

MILLER, P., and JOHNSON, T. (Eds.) *The Puritans: A Sourcebook of Their Writings*. New York: Harper and Row, 1963.

MILLER, S. M. "Comparative Social Mobility." *Current Sociology*, 1960, *9*.

MILNER, M., JR. "The Effects of Federal Aid to Higher Education on Social Inequality." Unpublished doctoral dissertation, Columbia University, 1970. Slightly different versions appeared as *Effects of Federal Aid to Higher Education on Social and*

Educational Inequality. New York: Center for Policy Research, 1970, and as Part I of *Higher Education in an Active Society: A Policy Study.* Washington, D.C.: Bureau of Social Science Research, Inc., 1970 (ERIC ED 040 695).

MILNER, M., JR. "Race, Education, and Jobs: Trends 1960–1970." Unpublished paper read at Eastern Sociological Association, New York, April 23–25, 1971.

NASH, G. "Student Financial Aid—College and University." Unpublished article written for the projected fourth edition of the *Encyclopedia of Educational Research* (Macmillan).

NIXON, R. M. Higher Education Message. Washington, D.C.: Office of the White House Press Secretary, March 19, 1970.

OSTOW, M. "Affiliation Contracts." In E. Ginzberg, *Urban Health Services: The Case of New York.* New York: Columbia University Press, 1970.

PECHMAN, J. A. "The Distributional Effects of Public Higher Education in California." *Journal of Human Resources,* 1970, *5,* 361–370.

Project TALENT. *One Year Follow-Up Study.* Cooperative research project 2333. Pittsburgh: University of Pittsburgh, 1966.

ROSE, A. M. "The Concept of Class in American Sociology." *Social Research,* 1958, *25,* 53–69.

SEWELL, W. H. "Inequality of Opportunity for Higher Education." *American Sociological Review,* 1971, *36,* 793–809.

SEWELL, W. H., and SHAH, V. P. "Socioeconomic Status, Intelligence, and the Attainment of Higher Education." *Sociology of Education,* 1967, *40,* 1–23.

SEWELL, W. H. "Students and the University." *The American Sociologist,* 1971, *6,* 111–112.

SHARP, L. *Two Years After the College Degree.* Washington, D.C.: Government Printing Office, 1963.

SIEGEL, P. M. "On the Cost of Being a Negro." *Sociological Inquiry,* 1965, *35,* 41–57.

SOLTOW, L. *Six Papers on the Size and Distribution of Wealth and Income.* New York: Columbia University Press, 1969.

SOWELL, T. "Increasing Misery." *American Economic Review,* 1960, *50,* 111–120.

SPADY, W. "Educational Mobility and Access: Growth and Paradoxes." *American Journal of Sociology,* 1967, *73,* 273–286.

SPAETH, J. L. "The Allocation of College Graduates to Graduate and Professional Schools." *Sociology of Education*, 1968, *41*, 342–349.

SUSSMAN, L. "Democratization and Class Segregation in Puerto Rican Schooling: US Model Transplanted." *Sociology of Education*, 1968, *41*, 321–341.

TAWNEY, R. H. *Equality*. (4th ed.) London: Unwin Books, 1964.

TOCQUEVILLE, A. DE. *Democracy In America*. Garden City, N.Y.: Doubleday, 1969.

US Bureau of the Census. "Educational Attainment." *Current Population Reports, P–20* (138, 158, 169, 182, 194).

US Bureau of the Census. "Income in 1967 of Families in the United States." *Current Population Reports, P–60* (59).

US Bureau of the Census. "Income in 1970 of Families and Persons in the United States." *Current Population Reports, P–60* (80).

US Bureau of the Census. "Men with College Degrees: March 1967." *Current Population Reports, P–20* (180).

US Bureau of the Census. "School Enrollment: October 1968 and 1967." *Current Population Reports, P–20* (190).

US Bureau of the Census. *Statistical Abstract of the United States, 1968, 1969, 1970.* Washington, D.C.: Government Printing Office 1968, 1969, 1970.

US Department of Health, Education, and Welfare. *Toward a Long-Range Plan for Federal Financial Support for Higher Education.* Washington, D.C.: Government Printing Office, 1969.

US Department of Labor. "Educational Attainment of Workers." *Special Labor Force Reports* (30, 63, 83, 92, 103, 125).

US Office of Education. *Digest of Educational Statistics.* Washington, D.C.: Government Printing Office, 1968, 1969, 1970.

US Office of Education. *Students and Buildings.* Washington, D.C.: Government Printing Office, 1968.

WEBER, M. "Class, Status, and Party." In *From Max Weber: Essays in Sociology*. New York: Oxford University Press, 1946.

WEBER, M. *The Theory of Social and Economic Organizations*. New York: Macmillan, 1947.

WEGNER, E. L. "Some Factors in Obtaining Postgraduate Education." *Sociology of Education*, 1969, *42*, 154–169.

WELTER, R. *Popular Education and Democratic Thought in America.* New York: Columbia University Press, 1962.

WERTS, C. "Career Changes in College." *Sociology of Education*, 1967, *40*, 90–95.

WERTS, C. "Path Analysis: Testimony of a Proselyte." *American Journal of Sociology*, 1968, *73*, 509–512.

WERTS, C. "Social Class and Initial Career Choice of College Freshmen." *Sociology of Education*, 1966, *39*, 348–358.

WOLFLE, D. L. "Educational Opportunity, Measured Intelligence, and Social Background." In A. H. Halsey, J. Floud, and C. A. Anderson (Eds.) *Education, Economy, and Society*. New York: Macmillan, 1961.

YANOWITCH, M. "The Soviet Income Revolution." *Slavic Review.* 1963, *22*, 683–697.

Index

A

Achievement, rewards for, 19–20
Achievement and equality: conflicts in, 20; conflicts in educational system about, 23–24; relationship between, 11–20
ADAMS, W., 83, 85
American Council on Education, 52, 63, 83
American ideals and values, contradictions in, 11–16
American people: chosen, vulnerable, and excluded, 2–4, 105–108; frustration and weariness of, 1–5, 28, 29
ASTIN, H. S., 45, 49, 50, 52, 55, 61, 67n, 67–68

B

Basic rights of citizens, expansion of, 152–156
BAYER, A. E., 45, 49, 50, 52, 55, 61, 67–68
BELL, D., 123n
BEN-DAVID, J., 148

BENDIX, R., 99–101, 101n, 102n, 111
BERDIE, R. F., 49
BERG, I., 120n
BERGER, B., 121
BIRNBAUM, R., 62
Blacks: academic ability of, 85–86; and the black revolution, 129–136; civil rights movement and militancy of, 135–136; discriminatory hiring and promotion of, 75, 80, 81, 82, 86–87; education as source of social status among, 84–85; impact of education on racial inequality of, 74–91; infant mortality and life expectancy figures for, 131–134; occupational status of following college, 79–82, 130–135; self-image of, 83–84; vs. whites in income, jobs, level of education, 75–79, 86; in World War II and Vietnam war, 135–136
BLAU, P. M., 56, 71–72, 101–104, 111
BOTTOMORE, T. B., 104, 111
BRONFENBRENNER, U., 145n

167

Index